CARS

MARTIN GURDON

© Haynes Publishing 2019
First published 2013
This edition published July 2019

A CIP Catalogue record for this book
is available from the British Library.

ISBN: 978 1 78521 584 1 (print)
ISBN: 978 1 78521 631 2 (eBook)

Library of Congress control no. 2019934668

Published by Haynes Publishing,
Sparkford, Yeovil, Somerset BA22 7JJ
Tel: 01963 440635
Int. tel: +44 1963 440635
Website: www.haynes.com

Printed in Malaysia.

Bluffer's Guide®, Bluffer's® and Bluff Your Way®
are registered trademarks.

Series Editor: David Allsop.
Design and Illustration: With thanks to Giles Chapman.

CONTENTS

For some, cars are giant, shiny badges of machismo or material success.
For others, they have become an everyday adjunct to life, as necessary as dental work but slightly more fun.

START ENGINES

Whether you regard them as expressions of your libido or extensions of your overdraft, cars are hard to ignore.

They're the subject of politics, lust, envy, aspiration and necessity. They're symbols of liberation and progress that stop you getting where you want to go as their numbers have multiplied like super-viruses and clogged up the roads.

Cars are the result of genius, megalomania, vanity and insanity, and have the capacity to both fascinate and bore. Visit one of Britain's few remaining pubs and in the corner of the bar will be a man with a brown nylon tie and his own tankard who knows everything about the Triumph Herald. Go to the car park of your local supermarket after it's shut and you'll find spotty boys in hoodies and saggy-arsed jeans who wish Jeremy Clarkson was their dad. They'll have memorised the top speed of every Lamborghini built since 1998, but have to content themselves with wheel-spinning a 12-year-old, wheezing, 1000cc Vauxhall Corsa until one of its drive shafts snap or they collect a shopping trolley as a bonnet mascot. Or both.

Car bluffing starts early, and the high cost of motoring is hardly a disincentive to drive. If you're under 25, then your first car will cost many times more than it's worth to insure for a year, sadly not because miserable, middle-aged insurers are jealous of your youth and vitality but because they reckon (with some justification) that you're an adrenalin-addled nutter who will wrap it round a Bentley at the first opportunity.

But this won't put you off car ownership. Quite the contrary. It will make the prospect of getting behind the wheel of your own car even more alluring. And you will remember that seminal moment for the rest of your life. Indeed, you can still recall those looks of admiring envy from other car owners when you first screeched to a halt on that garage forecourt, narrowly missing the tiers of wilting flowers and charcoal briquettes, as you casually stepped out of your wheezing runabout, and struck a noble pose of devil-may-care insouciance.

With the myopia of youth, you will have failed to notice that your audience's lips were collectively mouthing the word 'tosser', but no matter. You were finally there, you had joined the brother/sisterhood of car owners, and the road of freedom stretched out ahead of you with all its shimmering promise of limitless adventure.

For some, cars are giant, shiny badges of machismo or material success. For others, they have become an everyday adjunct to life, as necessary as dental work but slightly more fun.

Then there are car enthusiasts, for whom anything with a wheel at each corner is utterly fascinating. They can tell you the split-second speed with which a Porsche sequential transmission changes gear, or the flammability of the fibreglass used to make a Reliant Robin and how long it will take to burn one to the ground.

These people can be found at racetracks, bars, used-car lots, playgrounds and online, discussing head-spinning motoring minutiae that excludes those who aren't in the know. And that is where this short but definitive guide comes in. It sets out to conduct you through the main danger zones encountered in discussions about cars, and to equip you with a vocabulary and evasive technique that will minimise the risk of being rumbled as a bluffer. It will give you a few easy-to-learn hints and methods designed to ensure that you will be accepted as a car aficionado of rare ability and experience. But it will do more. It will provide you with the tools to impress legions of marvelling listeners with your knowledge and insight – without anyone discovering that, before reading it, you didn't know the difference between locknuts and recirculating balls, or a gudgeon pin and a big end. The first speeding ticket was issued to one Walter Arnold for driving at 8mph in a 2mph zone. If that law still stood today, you could get nicked for jogging.

The first speeding ticket was issued to one Walter Arnold for driving at 8mph in a 2mph zone. If that law still stood today, you could get nicked for jogging.

THE WHEELS OF TIME

You can't profess to be an expert on cars unless you have some grasp of their history. So sit down, relax and slip into neutral. Here's a short timeline of the evolution of the motor car.

1885 – THE BIRTH OF THE PETROL-POWERED AUTOMOBILE

The first really recognisable petrol car was revealed in 1885 by a German engineer called Karl Benz. With his walrus moustache and prominent ears, Benz looked as if he'd stepped from a cartoon in an early issue of *Punch* magazine. His car was a tricycle with solid tyres, one wheel at the front and a thumping engine under the seat. It looked like the progeny of a pram and a pony and trap, but without the pony.

Benz was one of a number of engineers working on horseless carriages, but his design was the first one that really worked properly.

To prove that there's never anything new, a

Frenchman, Étienne Lenoir, had already made the Hippomobile, a giant, hydrogen gas-powered three-wheeler way back in 1860. It looked a bit like a cattle-feeding trough on wheels but was a very early precursor to the fuel-cell cars that today's carmakers are spending billions trying to perfect to replace diesel- and petrol-engined vehicles, since the only thing they emit is water vapour. The Hippomobile wasn't ideal transport for people in a hurry, taking almost three hours to cover 11 miles – although that would be considered a good rate of progress in London today.

Another French inventor, Gustave Trouvé, had come up with a three-wheeled electric tricycle in 1881, having already thought up ideas for telephones, microphones and what was probably the first outboard motor for a boat (most of which, with the possible exception of the outboard, remained unfulfilled).

So why did the world end up with petrol rather than gas or electric cars? Well, the technology developed more quickly for internal combustion power and got progressively better. The infrastructure for fixing and fuelling these cars was established, but, to start with, finding fuel really limited the usability of early cars – though chemists did often sell it, alongside prophylactics and hair cream ('Going somewhere nice for the weekend, sir?'). In addition, early automobiles didn't need to carry hefty batteries filled with acid, could be refuelled quickly and didn't require hours of charging – a problem that true electric cars still have today.

Mind you, both electric and steam cars held the first land-speed world records, with the French Jeantaud electric car achieving an eye-watering 39.24mph in 1898. The following year, the company managed almost 66mph, and in 1902 a steam car called the Gardner-Serpollet 'Easter Egg' reached 75mph, which must have been terrifying, although nowhere near as buttock-clenchingly petrifying as the 127.659mph managed by Fred Marriott in the Stanley Rocket steam car on Daytona Beach, USA, in 1906.

Why would any sane person wedge himself into a confined space shared with a furnace and a lot of boiling water, and hurtle down a beach at over 100mph? Fred's explanation is unrecorded, but he managed to survive another 50 years, dying at the age of 83 in 1956.

Why would any sane person wedge himself into a confined space shared with a furnace and a lot of boiling water, and hurtle down a beach at over 100mph?

Early road cars could only be afforded by the rich and privileged classes. They cost a fortune to buy and maintain, with costly things like solid rubber tyres lasting only a few hundred miles.

Pneumatic, inflatable tyres had been around since 1846 but only really became practical in 1887, thanks to a lustrously bearded Scottish chap called John Boyd

Dunlop, who improved the design so that his sickly son could cycle in comfort. A lot of British bicycle makers were based in the Midlands, which explains why many car producers set up in that part of the world (because the skills and materials were near at hand), although early car-making workshops sprang up all over the place.

1896 – THE FIRST SPEEDING TICKET

Road cars were legally able to go faster as they no longer needed someone walking in front of them carrying a red flag, and could achieve speeds of 12mph without being caught out by early speed daguerreotype cameras (actually, that last bit's made up). But the following year, the first headlights appeared along with various types of audible warning, namely, a klaxon or horn. Continental motorists have never looked back because, as everyone knows, they love blowing their horns for no discernible reason.

Despite this, the first speeding ticket was issued to one Walter Arnold for driving at 8mph in a 2mph zone. If that law still stood today, you could get nicked for jogging.

1896 was also the year that cars started killing people. The first victim in Britain was Bridget Driscoll of Croydon, who was mown down in the grounds of Crystal Palace by a demonstration automobile travelling at a reckless 4mph (although a terrified passenger said it could have been as much as 8mph).

1906 – ROAD TRAFFIC LAW AND INSTITUTIONS

By 1906 the AA had arrived in the UK; followed swiftly by car insurance (not mandatory until later), number plates, vehicle registration, driving licences (although still no driving test), road signs, the first Rolls-Royce and, in the USA, the first filling station.

1907 – THE LAUNCH OF THE FORD MODEL T

When Henry Ford launched his Model T, nicknamed 'Tin Lizzie', most cars were recognisably car-shaped, with an engine at the front – unless they were Hillman Imps or Volkswagen Beetles, which hadn't yet been invented.

An important piece of a bluffer's impress-your-friends Model T-related trivia is that in 1921 it was possibly the first car to be offered with a child seat, even if the 'seat' was little more than a bit of sackcloth with a drawstring.

Ford, who later became famous for his mix of philanthropy and ruthlessness (he had a private army to sort out industrial disputes), had a knack for taking engineering ideas and making them work properly, and he came up with moving assembly lines from observing automated meat-packing plants in Chicago. State firmly that this was not only the end of the beginning but also the beginning of the end for car workers in the UK.

Mind you, if anyone tells you that Ford invented the mass-production process with the Model T, you can smugly point to the 1902 Oldsmobile Curved Dash, which looked more like a wheeled musical box than a car but was definitely the first mass-produced automobile.

Ford hugely sped up and brought down the cost of car production. He could make more cars for less money and the Model T, to use that tired old cliché, put America on wheels, with its original price falling from $850 to $260 by the mid-1920s.

Ford was obsessed with the materials his cars were made from and started using vanadium steel, which was strong, light and flexible, and helped make the Model T as tough as old boots. It needed to be, given the extremes of temperature in the USA and the often awful dirt roads with which its high ground clearance coped admirably.

To a lesser extent this applied in the UK, where tarmac was a luxury many roads didn't have, so fast-moving cars enveloped their occupants and pedestrians with Mr Toad-like swirls of dust and muck. Many occupants of cars wisely opted to wear special protective clothes and headwear.

Most cars eventually acquired things like roofs and glass windows, but it was still necessary to climb outside to get them going with a crank handle; electric starters didn't arrive until 1912.

1914 – THE FIRST WORLD WAR

At the outbreak of war in 1914, the industrialised world discovered industrialised warfare – in which motor vehicles played their part. And when that finished four years later, the US car giants were even better at making stuff because they'd had a lot of practice supporting the war effort. Even though they came to it late (as usual).

In Europe, things were tougher. Infrastructure and economies suffered lasting damage but countless entrepreneurs in the UK, France, Italy and Germany nonetheless all had a go at making cheap, affordable vehicles.

1922 – THE APPEARANCE OF THE AUSTIN 7

By 1920 it was estimated that there were nearly 9 million cars and trucks in the USA and nearly 100,000 in the UK, some of them with electric rather than kerosene lights – so there was less excuse for running over people in the dark. Two years later, a Birmingham-based carmaker called Herbert Austin launched his own version of a car for the masses. Called the Austin 7, it cost £165 and was so successful that versions were built in France, and in Germany, where it was called the Dixi and was assembled by a company that would soon be known as BMW.

1927 – THE UNUSUAL DEMISE OF ISADORA DUNCAN

If people weren't by now aware of the perils associated with the motor car, as well as its undoubted pleasures, the well-documented garrotting of celebrated dancer Isadora Duncan in Nice, France, was a warning to car occupants everywhere not to let their scarves get tangled up in the rear wheels while wearing them, especially when the car is moving at some speed. Her death wasn't the only vehicle-related tragedy she experienced. Her two children drowned in 1913 when the car they were travelling in plunged over a bridge and into the Seine in Paris, and Duncan herself was seriously injured in car accidents in 1913 and 1924.

1928 – THE MORRIS MINOR

Morris Motors Limited successfully launched a rival to the Austin 7, called the Minor, which could be bought brand new for £125. Not to be confused with the later model of the same name designed by Alec Issigonis, 86,318 of them were sold before production finished in the early 1930s.

1930s – THE ADVENT OF HYDRAULIC BRAKES AND STEEL PANELS

By the late 1930s, with the Second World War looming, many cars were now fitted with hydraulic brakes that were marginally more effective than the rods and cables that drivers had been accustomed to relying on. This was the decade when the car really came of age. Roads got better, and the cars more reliable and safe, although they were often cold because heaters were still a luxury.

During the 1930s, traditional coach-working skills were still being used in car production, with wood and canvas still present in many car bodies. But these were gradually giving way to pressed steel panels, thanks to an American engineering genius called Edward Budd, whose foresight made cars lighter, stronger, safer and rounder, allowing car builders to create new automobile designs in the 1930s with a lot of sweeping art deco curves.

In 1934 Budd's ideas influenced the Citroën Traction Avant, a car famously favoured by Inspector Maigret, which, instead of having its body bolted onto a separate chassis frame like a carriage, had a welded structure that was all one piece (just like most modern cars), so it was lighter, lower, potentially stronger and ultimately cheaper to build.

It also had front-wheel drive – again, like many cars today – getting rid of all the gubbins that connected the engine to the back wheels and freeing up space in the cabin so that there was more room. In addition, being pulled round corners by its front wheels, rather than pushed by the back ones, helped with its roadholding.

Citroën wanted the Traction Avant – so named because of its front-wheel drive – to be convenient and easy to handle, and tried to do away with the clutch pedal, although without success. In fact, Citroën wanted the car to appeal to people who didn't particularly care about cars, especially women.

State confidently, with an air of *je ne sais quoi*, that the Traction Avant was a brilliant piece of industrial design.

Conceived before the Second World War as a German 'people's car', the Beetle's 'interesting' handling characteristics earned it the sobriquet of 'Hitler's Revenge'.

A SHORT INTERVAL

Some more historical background will be necessary before you can confidently venture an opinion on the evolution of motor cars. If in doubt, say that in the post-war era the Germans and the Japanese progressively exercised the biggest influence on automotive design, safety and reliability. Between 1939 and 1945, these two nations had ensured that people's minds were somewhat preoccupied with other matters, and after the industrialised world had been brought to its knees for a second time, carmakers sifted through the wreckage and picked up where they'd left off. The bluffer's position in all of this is to be gracious in victory and point out that more important things were at stake than manufacturing cars.

For a while during the immediate post-war years there was a short-lived rash of very tiny, very crude British economy cars, some of which were real stinkers. Take the Gordon, which cost £300 in 1954 and was Britain's cheapest car. It had one wheel at the front and two at the back. To perfect its inherent instability, the designers put its single-cylinder, 197cc motorcycle engine outside, next to the driver, who invariably suffered tinnitus in his or her right ear as a result. The engine was connected by chain to one back wheel. Bizarrely, this lethal-sounding confection was made by a subsidiary of Vernons Pools, which clearly had issues when it came to backing a winner.

In Italy, a fridge-maker invented the tiny Isetta bubble car, with one wheel at the back (or a pair of tiny wheels very close together) and a single door at the front over two further wheels. BMW, later to become makers of 'the ultimate driving machine', built a version of this, assembling it in an old railway workshop near Brighton.

Although many still had their doubts about the Germans, they grew to love the Volkswagen Beetle because it was robustly built and rarely went wrong.

And who could possibly forget the part the German-built Messerschmitt played in post-war car manufacturing? That would be the car, not the plane. Temporarily banned from building the latter, the German aircraft engineer Fritz Fend turned his hand to producing bubble cars which looked uncannily similar to a wingless version of the eponymous fighter plane, with no fuselage and just the cockpit and canopy on wheels. You should know that more than 40,000 of them were built between 1956 and 1964. Many a former RAF bomber pilot must have had a nasty shock when he saw one in the rear-view mirror of his Humber Hawk.

THE GERMAN RESURGENCE

Although many still had their doubts about the Germans, they grew to love the Volkswagen Beetle because it was robustly built and rarely went wrong.

Never mind that it sounded like a biological motion in a bathtub, or that thanks to having its engine dangling pendulously behind the back wheels, and an appropriately named 'swing-axle' suspension, it had an unfortunate habit of spinning and vanishing backwards through hedges at the slightest hint of a corner. Conceived before the Second World War as a German 'people's car', the Beetle's 'interesting' handling characteristics earned it the sobriquet of 'Hitler's Revenge'. But in 1971 that didn't stop the back-to-front Volkswagen overtaking the Ford Model T as the world's bestselling car.

THE SEAT BELT

As the age of 1950s austerity petered out and the Technicolor 1960s arrived, people began to remind themselves that cars could be dangerous. Although in 1885 New Yorker Edward J Claghorn had patented a belt 'designed to be applied to the person, and provided with hooks and other attachments for securing a person to a fixed object', it wasn't until 1959 that Volvo launched a car with the first standard three-point seat belt.

TURNING JAPANESE

The 1960s saw cars getting better, safer and more reliable – although a lot of unforgivable tat was still being sold. More people were making cars in more places, including Japan, but when the first Subarus, Daihatsus and Toyotas were exported, many established carmakers sniggered and dismissed these Asian upstarts. After all, who'd want to buy a Datsun Z sports car when they could have an MG, and why would Beetle lovers switch to the ultra-dull Toyota Corolla?

It transpired that quite a lot of people were willing to buy them, actually, doubtless beguiled by the twin prospects of reliability and value for money – not to mention having things like seat belts, headrests and radios as standard.

By the middle of the grimly beige 1970s, xenophobia and national pride were giving way to commercial pragmatism and Japanese cars were suddenly ubiquitous. Volkswagen nearly went bust sticking with the Beetle when buyers weren't, and only just saved its skin in 1974 by building the first Golf, whose front-engine, front-drive, mid-sized hatchback layout became the template for Europe's most successful car category.

Over forty years on, VW still makes a car called a Golf that has all of these features – and so do most of its rivals.

SAFETY FIRST

In 1968 American engineer Allen Breed patented the airbag, and by the mid-1970s US cars started to be fitted with it – despite a retired safety engineer suggesting that the airbag's capacity for breaking an unsecured person's neck would make it a very effective alternative to the electric chair.

Exhaust catalysts also appeared in the USA. These glorified filth-filters sifted some of the nasty, chemical soot that car engines belched out. Because they used precious metals like platinum they were also expensive, and the first ones actually made engines use more fuel (thus producing more CO_2, the world's favourite greenhouse gas). They were a mixed blessing.

It took quick-thinking, engine-controlling computers to address this inefficiency during the 1980s, but it would take another 20 years or so for features like anti-lock brakes and tension-activated seat belts to become universal features.

OVERTAKING

All the while, bigger carmakers were ingesting smaller or less successful ones with an amoeba-like enthusiasm, which reached its apex in the early 2000s and was driven by a mix of economies of scale and a hegemonistic culture among motor industry executives that would have impressed Alexander the Great.

Visit an international, early 2000s motor show and you'd have seen ever-more grandiose stands where car producers lined up all the smaller brands they'd bought. Ford could jeer at DaimlerChrysler, pointing at its Jaguars, Aston Martins, Volvos and Mazdas, but Mercedes could jeer back with serried rows of Chryslers,

Jeeps, Dodges and Smart cars on a stand that was bigger than everyone else's.

Volkswagen could wave two fingers at the opposition with an array of Audis, Škodas, SEATs, Bugattis, Lamborghinis and Bentleys (which, admittedly, wasn't a bad haul), and Peugeot shrugged its shoulders and pointed to Citroën, which it had acquired way back in 1974 and with admirable Gallic insouciance couldn't be bothered to crow about. Meanwhile, Fiat had sucked up Ferrari a few years before that, and could notch up Maserati and Alfa Romeo among its subsequent conquests.

Rolls-Royce had eaten Bentley way back in the 1930s, but when the joint firm was sold, there was a tug of love between Volkswagen and BMW in 1998, which left VW with Bentley and BMW with the Rolls-Royce name but no factory to make the cars, so it built a brand-new one in the grounds of the Goodwood Estate in Sussex.

BMW's other master stroke was to buy Rover. This proved so indigestible that it flogged the company to some ex-Rover bosses for a tenner. Scandalously, having depicted themselves as 'white knights', the so-called Phoenix Four proceeded to feather their own nests as it went bust.

Cleverly, BMW hung on to the Mini bit of Rover, building a new, hugely successful version of the car at the Cowley factory in Oxford that had once made Morris Minors.

Subsequently, a lot of carmakers who bought their rivals sold them off again, as the executives who'd done this were sacked, got new jobs or retired. So Mercedes-Benz flogged Chrysler to Fiat, not long after Ford kissed goodbye to Aston Martin, Jaguar, Land Rover and Volvo, managing to avoid bankruptcy in the process. General Motors, which owned Vauxhall since the 1920s, has flogged both it and Germany's Opel (same cars, different badges) to Peugeot. Thus Vauxhall's weirdly named Grandland X is actually a Peugeot 3008 in disguise.

RELATIVE VALUES

These days, cars aren't what they seem.

Hyundai is a South Korean company, but a lot of its cars are made in the Czech Republic and Turkey. Kia, another South Korean manufacturer, builds cars in Slovakia.

There's a Renault 4x4 almost nobody buys called the Koleos that's made in South Korea. Lots of Hondas, Toyotas and Nissans are built in the UK. Volkswagen-owned 'Spanish' SEATs have been assembled in Germany, while 'German' VWs are made in South Africa and exported back to Europe.

If you buy a Toyota Aygo, a Citroën C1 or a Peugeot 107 baby car, they all come from the same Czech factory because they're all the same car with different badges and a few styling tweaks. Ditto the Nissan Pixo and Suzuki Alto, two 'Japanese' cars built on the same production line in India. Rival cars are often more closely related than you'd imagine or their makers advertise. Take the reborn Fiat 500, which begat its innards to the Mk2 Ford Ka, saving Ford the cost of designing these things themselves. And any Volvo V40 owner who feels superior to someone with a Ford Focus should be made to squirm with the knowledge that both cars are much the same underneath.

IDENTITY ISSUES

Increasingly, cars – especially if they're small and cheap – are built in parts of the world where people get paid less because a little car has very nearly as many bits as a big, expensive one, so screwing a profit from it is harder.

For people who care about such things and can afford them, the places where exotic cars are made are still part of their appeal, which means that the Indian and Chinese ultra-rich who now bankroll Bentley, Ferrari, et al. by buying their shiny products, still want them to be made by tea-swilling Brits in exotic Crewe or pasta-loving Italians in Modena. Made anywhere else, these things would be like fake Rolex watches. In fact, China is home to an impressive number of counterfeit cars, including not-quite copies of the BMW X5 4x4 and Daimler AG's Smart car, which led the makers of the originals to consult m'learned friends.

Perversely, Communist China has become the largest market for BMW's biggest, poshest model, the 7-Series saloon, and cars like this and the equally plutocratic Audi A6 are also manufactured there, along with cars from emerging Chinese producers like Baolong, Foton, Chery, BYD and Changan (some of whose badges look remarkably similar to those of well-known German and Japanese competitors). Then there's truck manufacturer Dadi Auto with a range of Japanese-styled SUVs which look strangely familiar, the deeply catchy tractor manufacturer Dongfeng with a range of equally familiar-looking passenger saloons, the modestly named Brilliance China Automotive of minibus-making fame, and former fridge manufacturer Geely which now owns a sleepy European carmaker called Volvo.

There are now an estimated 144 million cars in China, creating a lot of snarl-ups. In one six-month period, 9,598,000 were sold, according to previously published figures on the ChinaAutoWeb website. China now makes more new cars than any other country, so if you're looking for obscure pub quiz questions, this will be heartening news.

And there's India's Tata, which controls what's left of Britain's steel industry. It makes its own cars but also owns Jaguar and Land Rover (now called Jaguar Land Rover); and, unlike Ford, which oversaw both, and BMW, which bankrolled Land Rover for a bit, has actually made money from them.

India's roads are still choked up with smoke-belching Tata buses and trucks, and the omnipresent motor rickshaw trikes, but its new car population is expanding, with up to 70 million vehicles on the road already and predictions of 450 million in 20 years, helped perhaps by this century's first true 'people's car'. Called the Tata Nano and designed to get Indian families off little motorcycles and into slightly less tiny cars, it costs the equivalent of just under £1,600.

If it succeeds and India's car population explodes, Nano owners could end up having plenty of time to admire their dinky little cars – parked nose to tail in the world's biggest traffic jam.

B

Now, France has some of Europe's best roads, which means that manufacturers have taken their eye off the virtues of a great French 'ride', and most of its cars now ride like the horse-drawn tumbrel carts of the French Revolution.

INTERNATIONAL CHARACTERISTICS

Cars used to have obvious national idiosyncrasies, but they have become harder to define with the increasingly global homogenisation of manufacturing and design. Yet there are still some decorative hints and driving habits that reflect certain countries and their cultures. You not only need to know what these are, but you also need the backstory as to why they endure.

FRANCE

French cars were, for a while in the 1960s and 1970s, *la plus haute aspiration* for British drivers numbed by the stunningly dreary offerings of their own national car industry. For years French cars had softer rides than models made in other countries, as well as sometimes endearingly quirky appearances. Utility cars like the Renault 4 and Citroën 2CV might both have looked like suitcases on wheels, but they had extraordinarily comfortable suspension and drove like sofas – an essential prerequisite because of some uniformly awful French roads.

This also meant that while a lot of French cars rolled like drunken matelots when they went round corners, that didn't stop many of them doing this better than any other car. Now, France has some of Europe's best roads, which means that manufacturers have taken their eye off the virtues of a great French 'ride', and most of its cars now ride like the horse-drawn tumbrel carts of the French Revolution.

For years a lot of French cars looked wilfully odd, and had yellow headlights so they stood out even in the dark. Later, the headlamps became white like everyone else's and many of the designs got quite bland, although Renault went very peculiar with its bustle-backed Mégane, which had a boot shaped like a monkey's arse in a metal crinoline – a look the company has wisely since abandoned.

But whatever you say about French cars, they once had a distinctive identity. Models such as the Citroën DS and the Peugeot 404 Cabriolet were more unmistakeably French than Gérard Depardieu (before he became a Russian), but today the most likely national characteristic of a French car is that it will have a diesel engine. Otherwise it is so lacking in identity that it could be German, or South Korean, or frankly – who cares? And to think that the mass-production Citroën DS was once voted by *Classic & Sports Car* magazine as the most beautiful car of all time.

GERMANY

Despite BMW wigging out a bit style-wise in recent years, German cars generally have a sober aesthetic, with clean lines and easy-to-spot visual iconography (Mercedes and BMW grilles can't really be mistaken for anything else).

A lot of German cars are sold on the subtle marketing premise that they are better made than their French or Italian equivalents, even if this isn't necessarily true, and a lot of their appeal is about one-upmanship. This means that the more expensive the German car, often the more buttons, lights and buzzers it will have. Indeed, the Porsche Panamera, a huge saloon resembling a 911 that's been sat on by an elephant, has a button for absolutely everything.

German cars always come with huge instruction books with more badly written words than a Dan Brown thriller. They are also often very bossy, more or less warning hapless owners that they face imprisonment if they forget to check the tyre pressures.

Frequently the cars themselves are just as prescriptive, pinging audible warnings and flashing instructions at their owners for every possible misdemeanour.

Because Germany has had Autobahn motorways since the 1930s, some of which still have no speed limits, a lot of its cars can be driven flat out for hours on end without blowing up, and have firm, not to say hard, rides because potholes are forbidden.

This characteristic is enhanced by the German car-making habit of fitting wide wheels and very stiff, low-profile tyres to their cars, which give them sometimes eyeball-rattling rides on less forgiving British roads.

ITALY

Even the cheapest Italian cars used to have a distinctive verve and panache to compensate for a tendency to rot away in minutes and a habit of stuffing electrics like knotted tagliatelle haphazardly behind door panels.

This is a country where car style has always been infinitely more desirable than ensuring that the things start or stop. Generations of blokes have looked at Italian cars and gone 'Phwoaaar!', which perhaps explains why it's the home of Ferrari and Maserati, makers of some of the world's fastest and most sensuous exotic cars. Even cheap cars like the old, rear-engined Fiat 500 Cinquecento had a cute, unthreatening pertness that rivalled and, some would say, outmatched the Mini.

Italy is a country where car style has always been infinitely more desirable than ensuring that the things start or stop.

More recently, Italian cars have grown up. They're not especially prone to rust, and their electrics seem to have improved, too, but despite some still-dashing styling, many of the less exotic supercars have lost their characteristic air of *la dolce vita* and no longer feel distinctively Italian. Of course, this is a mixed blessing, as part of that feeling once used to involve an excessive degree of mechanical frailty.

There's also a residual sense that Italians love dreaming up cars and driving them, but the day-in, day-out monotony of actually building and servicing them remains a bit of a chore, and as a result their cars still aren't quite as well screwed together as German or Japanese ones.

USA

The USA is such a vast country that a lot of cars that appear to be foreign imports are actually made there because it's cheaper than shipping them over. These include Honda, Toyota, BMW and Mercedes models, which these days look indistinguishable from their Japanese and German counterparts.

Basically, a lot of US cars, including such familiar names as Chevrolets, Dodges and Cadillacs, have shrunk – as indeed has the country's auto industry. Things don't look too promising when Detroit, aka 'Motor City', is fighting off bankruptcy with debts of $18 billion, a population that has dwindled to a third of what it was in its 1960s heyday, and thousands of shops and houses abandoned and derelict.

But some parts of the US car industry remain seemingly impervious to economic realities. The pickup truck is alive and well. Some are capable of accommodating an extended American family and enough construction materials for a small town. These road beasts, with subtle names like Ram or Silverado, are almost lorry-sized and boast lorry-style engineering, with massive engines and sub-structures made from steel girders capable of supporting an office building.

With giant freeways and plenty of space, US cars had historically grown and grown. Many were pretty crudely engineered, had seats like armchairs, and velour and leatherette-lined interiors with all the subtle appeal of a strip club. They handled like three-legged camels but were surprisingly relaxing when covering vast distances in straight lines which, most of the time, is what they did.

By European standards the average US car is increasingly astoundingly good value and laden with kit, but one thing that sets even their most prestigious marques apart from their non-American rivals is the way they feel inside.

There's something about the plastics and fabrics used that feels, well, more Walmart than Waitrose; you can even smell the difference. The USA is the home of mass-produced consumer durables, and that's something that the insides of its cars still won't let you forget.

JAPAN

Here's another country where a distinctive automotive national identity has been subsumed into something, well, bland.

In the past, Japanese cars were easily identifiable because they were made from reclaimed, imported steel which went horribly rusty, but they very rarely went wrong because they were mechanically bulletproof.

Many from the late 1960s to the late 1970s looked vaguely like scaled-down US cars, with madly chintzy interiors decked out with weird little crests and swirly patterns embossed on their plastic headrests – but customers put up with nonsense like this because the headrests were standard, unlike their rivals.

In a world where the likes of Ford sometimes charged extra for a passenger sun visor, a perma-reliable Japanese car with tinted glass and an AM/FM radio had a lot of appeal, even if it looked fussy on the outside, mad on the inside and, thanks to often very basic engineering and steering, was pretty ropey to drive.

Despite the derivative nature of much period Japanese car styling, many of these early machines had a curiously Oriental appearance. This had something to do with window, light and grille shapes, and it's fair to say that many Japanese cars do appear to have faces – apparently quite deliberately.

These days, with leading designers engaged in global career bed-hopping from one carmaker to the next, and Japanese – and, more recently, South Korean – car producers setting up design studios in the USA and Europe, this design trait has been watered down as cars have become increasingly internationalised. But unearth a Japanese city car and it will look like nothing else. There's a big market for models, known as Kei cars, that are under 1.48m wide and 3.4m long with engines no bigger than 660cc. Cars like the Nissan Roox and Toyota Pixis Space often resemble cardboard boxes on which surprised faces have been drawn – and really couldn't come from anywhere else.

UK

Would it be very unkind to say that the average 'British' car is made by a Japanese car producer? Toyota, Honda and Nissan all have long-established British factories and churn out vehicles by the hundreds of thousands, but there's nothing very British about any of them, other than the people who ensure that they roll off the production line.

Ford still makes diesel engines in the UK, but all the vehicles they go in are built elsewhere – like Spain and Germany. Vauxhall makes cars in Ellesmere Port, but they are mostly designed and engineered in Germany. Since the mid-1970s, most Vauxhalls have been designed in Germany by its sister company Opel. Both were owned by the American giant General Motors which, incidentally, took over Vauxhall in 1925, but has since taken its baseball bat home and sold Vauxhall and Opel to Peugeot.

A lot of Jaguars and Land Rovers are made just up the road from Ellesmere Port in exotic Halewood, at a factory that once assembled Ford Escorts. Although both brands cheerfully trade on past glories, their products have ditched the tweedy and Barbour-jacket-wearing country landowner image with which they were once synonymous. The average new Jaguar or Land Rover is an entirely modern 'lifestyle choice', and comes to you courtesy of a giant Indian steel conglomerate.

German-owned Rolls-Royce's current, mostly vast saloons and convertibles have slab-sided styling that mixes the visual brutality of a Stalinist office block with visual winks and nods to the Rolls models of the 1950s and 1960s – ensuring that the car stands out in Moscow or Shanghai, which are both places where you're most likely to see one. Inside, there's a modernist take on the leather-lined, wood-veneer-panelled, private club drawing room look that the car made its own for generations. But in recent years all the under-the-surface plastics and fire-retardant materials have meant that Rolls has had to find ways to make its interiors smell as if they're made from walnut trees and cowhide rather than industrial extrusions.

Bugatti's cars were motoring's equivalent of Hollywood film stars, and one in particular was a sort of Rudolph Valentino on wheels.

VISIONARY PETROLHEADS

The car industry has attracted all sorts of people, from artists, visionaries and business experts to delusional knaves. Some have been geniuses, some thought they were geniuses but were in fact profoundly mistaken, others had massive egos for no very good reason, and still others were tyrants whose tyranny was tolerated because they were often right. Here, in no particular order, is a selection – although don't expect any of them to be female. Women have got more sense.

ETTORE BUGATTI

Born in Milan in 1881, Bugatti was an inspired designer whose original cars mixed art and engineering in equal measure, coupled with an often left-field approach to design. In fact, his very first vehicle, a tricycle he built in his teens, had two engines.

Perhaps his aesthetic sensibilities were shaped by his father, Carlo, who trained as an architect, and designed and crafted fabulous art nouveau furniture and musical instruments. Ettore's grandfather, Giovanni Luigi, was a sculptor, as was Ettore's brother, Rembrandt (not that one), whose representations of exotic animals are still highly prized.

Bugatti's approach was that if something looked right, it usually was, and his cars had a no-expense-spared mix of performance and aesthetic purity that made them instant collector's items. They were motoring's equivalent of Hollywood film stars, and one in particular was a sort of Rudolph Valentino on wheels. With its 12.7-litre, eight-cylinder engine and sensuous 21-foot length, the Bugatti Type 41 'Royale' was intended to appeal to European royalty, and 25 were planned. Thanks to the Great Depression of 1929, just six were made and none of them ended up with royal owners. During the Second World War, one was hidden in Parisian sewers to keep it from the Nazis. Ettore's own prized prototype, which didn't have headlamps because he never drove it at night, was bricked up for the same reason.

As if acknowledging the Royale's incongruity in a world of economic and social disaster, its radiator mascot was a rampant silver elephant – a representation of one of Rembrandt Bugatti's sculptures.

(**Don't say** 'Perhaps it should have been a white elephant.')

SIR ALEC ISSIGONIS

If Ettore Bugatti was an automotive engineer with a sense of visual theatre and occasionally tasteful excess, then the Greek-British car designer Sir Alec Issigonis, the man who thought up the post-war Morris Minor and the original Mini, made cars with all the frills and frippery of a Trappist monk's Christmas party. Oddly, that didn't stop them becoming design icons.

Despite creating two of the twentieth century's best-loved 'people's cars', the gaunt and ascetic Issigonis, who never married and lived at home with his mum, had an unconventional approach to draughtsmanship. He was said to have started designing the Mini by standing two pairs of chairs behind each other and drawing a chalk rectangle on the floor round them with enough space for a boot and the engine, which he turned sideways, with the gearbox underneath it to save space.

Issigonis wasn't known for his people or management skills. Maintaining that the public didn't know what it wanted, but that he did, he insisted that market research was 'bunk' and that hatchbacks were rubbish because chopping a big hole in the back of a car weakened its structure. Today the hatchback is Europe's most popular car body type, so he got that one badly wrong. Nonetheless, his aggressively utilitarian designs were vastly entertaining to drive and often handled far better than many contemporary sports cars, with exceptional steering and beautiful balance – in fact, the Mini was a fabulously successful rally car because of this.

Do say 'Issigonis didn't make cars to win races. His reasoning was that a car that handled well was safer than one that didn't. In his world, driving wasn't necessarily about fun.'

SYLVANUS F BOWSER

Some of motoring's bit players also deserve a mention, although American Sylvanus Freelove Bowser's contribution was in its way immense, because he invented the petrol pump and is therefore a precious nugget for bluffers to drop idly into conversations about motoring milestones.

Oddly enough, Bowser didn't realise what he'd come up with when he sold the first pump in 1885. His idea was to provide shopkeepers who sold kerosene for household lamps and stoves with a safer way of dispensing the stuff than the ladles generally used at the time.

One of his first customers was a general store owner named Jake Gumper, who took delivery of a pump with a wooden storage barrel, marble valves and a handle to pump the liquid. This device became known as a 'filling station', and within eight years Bowser was selling versions of it to the first car repair shops, which generally supplied fuel in five-gallon cans that car owners used to pour their fuel into the petrol tanks, using a gauze-lined funnel to remove impurities.

By 1905 the few cars that hadn't been incinerated by fuel being slopped onto their hot exhaust pipes were often refuelled somewhat haphazardly by the roadside, so Bowser refined his design once again, incorporating a rubber hose to allow the fuel to be discharged straight into tanks.

To this day in far-flung parts of the English-speaking world, fuel pumps are still known as 'Bowsers'.

Sylvanus's other inventions are said to have included back-scratching devices and 'a sit-down enema', which might have given rise to the expression 'Yowser!' – except that it didn't.

Do say 'Perhaps it's just as well that he never called his creation the "Freelove pump", after his middle name.'

FATHER ALFRED JULIANO

Cars have always attracted dreamers and unusual characters. Father Alfred Juliano, creator of the 1958 Aurora Safety Sedan, unquestionably the ugliest car ever built, is a case in point.

A Catholic priest from Connecticut, Alfred wanted to be a car designer before God called him, but finding that he couldn't quite give up the world of motoring, he began dreaming up a 'safety car'.

The result was the Aurora. It was 18 feet long with a body made from fibreglass, and had a greenhouse-like roof and windows made from clear perspex, including an extraordinary windscreen which looked like a Cro-Magnon forehead (intended to be pedestrian-friendly in a crash) and supposed aerodynamic properties that made windscreen wipers redundant. Seats that swivelled round in a collision might not have been a good idea, but seat belts, a collapsible steering column, a padded dashboard and a bumper section with foam inserts were actually ahead of their time.

Father Juliano constructed his outlandish creation using an old Buick, and the car broke down continually on the way to its public unveiling in New York. Orders were not forthcoming, and the good Father, who found himself under investigation for tax fraud, accused of filching his parishioners' donations, reportedly went bankrupt and was forced to give up his ministry.

By the early 1990s, Juliano had died but his weird creation lived on, rotting in a field behind a car body shop in the USA, from where it was eventually rescued by English custom-car builder Andy Saunders who famously said: 'It was so ugly it was unreal. I said straightaway, "I've got to own that."' He spent 12 years restoring it and the all-American folly now lives in Britain and was last heard of pulling in the crowds at the National Motor Museum at Beaulieu in Hampshire. **Do say** 'There was a certain perverse beauty in its hideousness. As the Scots say, everything has a right to be ugly, but this abused the privilege.'

SUCK, SQUASH, BANG AND BLOW

Few of us care what goes on under the bonnet of the car – unless, of course, the engine doesn't start when it's supposed to. But to have any bluffing credibility at all, you need to have a basic understanding of how it all works. These days, a car's inner workings are usually hidden behind a baffling-looking apparatus of plastic covers, boxes, wires, cables and pipes joining one mystery object to another.

However, if yours is a diesel- or petrol-powered car, the way automotive power is provided is pretty straightforward, even if describing the processes involved isn't. Basically, the fuel, which is highly combustible, is squirted into a confined space where it's set alight. This makes it explode, and the energy created drives the engine, which in turn drives the car.

Petrol is more willing to go bang than diesel, as any recidivist arsonist will attest, before setting light to it and being blown into the next postcode. This is known as external combustion and should not be attempted by anyone with half a brain. In the context of current petrol cars, what happens instead is internal combustion. Some petrol is squirted into a cylindrical space in the engine called a bore (as in 'bore hole'), where it's mixed with air – also sucked into the space with the help of valves that open and close at strategic moments – and the resultant vaporous cocktail is ignited by an electrical spark from something called a spark plug.

This produces a lot of energy. In fact, howstuffworks. com reckons that enough is made 'to propel a potato 500 feet', which is a deeply pointless thing to do.

Unlike the average man, a crankshaft can multitask.

Instead, the petrol/air vapour shares the bore with a 'piston', which sits very snugly and moves up and down inside it, helped by being attached by a pivot to a connecting rod.

(Don't worry, nearly there.) The other end of the connecting rod is attached by a second pivot, amusingly known as a 'big end', to a piece of heavy engineering called a crankshaft – which in profile looks like a Cubist drawing of the up and down lines on an oscilloscope – so when it goes round and round, the connecting rod goes up and down, forcing the piston to join in.

As the piston heads for the bottom of its travel, fuel and air are sucked into the space above it, which is then sealed by the valves, so that as the piston goes back up again, the fuel/air mixture is squashed, which means that when the spark plug sets light to it, a lot of pressure has built up and even more energy is released, forcing the piston down again, filling the bore with all those nasty gases produced by the explosion.

When the piston next heads to the top of the bore, a valve opens and this pushes the spent gas out and into the exhaust system, before starting the process all over again.

Cars have had anything from one to 16-plus cylinders, but most of them make do with four, and a single crank (to which all the pistons are attached) but at different points in the combustion cycle, so that they rhythmically bob up and down, taking turns to suck in the fuel and air, blow it up then chuck out the filth. Another way to think of it might be 'Suck/Squash/Bang/Blow!', but that sounds like an adult movie title and probably shouldn't be repeated in polite company.

Moving on, unlike the average man, a crankshaft can multitask, and one end of it is connected to a car's transmission, which in turn uses drive or propeller shafts to make the wheels go round and the car move.

Why do you need a transmission? Well, if you've ever ridden a bicycle you'll know that changing the gears impacts on how easy it is to ride, that lower gears help get it up hills without exhausting you, and higher ones allow it to go faster on the flat or downhill. This is what a car's transmission does, sometimes in a way that involves you deciding when it changes gear, or in some cases doing this for you, but this is digressing from the limitless bluffing potential of engines.

Diesel engines do much the same thing with the same bits as petrol ones but without spark plugs. Diesel, or heavy oil, is less prone to exploding than petrol and so the way diesel engines persuade the fuel to combust is to keep squashing it. If you've ever put your thumb over the end of a bicycle pump and pumped, you will know that compressing the air you've trapped will make it get hot. So a diesel power unit is officially known as a 'compression ignition' engine because it keeps squishing the fuel and air until they give up and set light to themselves.

When this happens, diesel generally burns more efficiently than petrol does and the combustion process is more complete, which is why diesels are normally more economical, and actually produce less CO_2, or 'greenhouse gas', than equivalent petrols. However, they spew forth thoroughly unpleasant soot particles, called particulates, requiring even more filtering and cleaning up. Carmakers claim to have this problem licked with their latest offerings (although they said that about their older ones), but the effectiveness of this filtration, particularly in ageing diesels, and the asthmatic and carcinogenic properties of their tailpipe emissions are amongst the reasons their fuel has been the subject of a sales and reputational backlash and why diesels are probably facing long-term extinction in towns.

This hasn't been helped by VW, once the car world's answer to Barack Obama, getting its diesel models' engine management computers to recognise when they're being tested for cleanliness in laboratories – particularly in America – and not delivering peak power (and peak filth) when made to work hard in test conditions, but polluting merrily when back on the open road. Thanks to this 'fake spews' software, VW now has the mother of all legal bills and a reputation more akin to Donald Trump's.

There are other forms of automotive power, including petrol/electric and diesel/electric hybrids, which have both petrol or diesel and electric motors and can switch between the two or use one or the other. (Just remember the word 'hybrid' and posit that they're a halfway house on the way to full electricity.) Then there are rotary petrol engines that only have three moving parts. Designed by a German called Felix Wankel (don't even think about it), they're smooth but often have an insatiable thirst, can be a bit dirty, and have been known to suffer from an early burnout as a result of frazzling their mechanical extremities.

And that's all there is to it. Simple, really.

Sometimes, especially if the car is German, it will shout at you, even when nothing is actually wrong.

WHAT'S THAT TICKING NOISE?

THE GOOD OLD DAYS

Cars don't break down as much as they used to and, most of the time, they don't break down in the same way.

If you were born in the 1960s or earlier you might remember endless motorway journeys where the tedium of being glued to a vinyl seat in something like a Ford Escort or a Vauxhall Victor could be marginally relieved by counting all the other cars broken down on the hard shoulder and wondering when yours would join them.

Like the corpses of flies at the bottom of a closed window, these sorry-looking casualties littered the roadside, bonnets up, owners poking about fruitlessly to try and find out why the damn things wouldn't go. Having failed to find out, they'd then trudge hundreds of yards along the hard shoulder, lungs and clothing irreparably damaged by the fume-enriched slipstreams of passing Foden trucks and rattling Royal Blue coaches, as they searched for a motorway emergency phone that, inevitably, wouldn't work.

In an era when everyone and their dog has a mobile phone and the ether fairly fizzes with electromagnetic pollution, this might seem especially anachronistic, but it was actually just part of normal, pre-1980s life. You should fondly recall it as a time when motoring was the 'real thing'.

THE END OF DIY

One reason why so many of them continually broke down was that fixing one's own car was a default setting for the majority of male drivers. In the first 30 years after the Second World War, many men had seen military service and had grown where 'make do and mend' was a necessity that resulted in a great deal of vehicular bodging, inherited from a soldiering culture where if your tank broke down you fixed it with a claw hammer, an empty can of bully beef and a safety pin.

Servicemen who returned to Civvy Street households that were lucky enough to own cars often didn't have sufficient cash to get them serviced, so at weekends on streets and driveways all over the country, blokes would be seen banging their heads on the undersides of bonnets of Morris Oxfords and Hillman Hunters, gashing themselves on sharp bits of engine, and cauterising their wounds on overheated spark plugs while simultaneously leafing through an oil-smudged Haynes manual (but not until they were first published in the 1960s). Often they would do these things with a lit Woodbine hanging out of the corner of their mouths – ill-advised when inhaling a dangerously combustible mixture of oxygen and petrol vapour.

If some nostalgia freak tells you that 'they don't make cars like they used to any more', agree at once, because it's true. But state knowledgeably that this is actually a good thing. Something called progress has made modern cars more complicated but also generally less lethal, wasteful and unreliable, so they now don't require mechanical poking and prodding every other weekend in the way that their forebears did.

THE OLD MECHANICAL VERNACULAR

However, this has removed a lot of the bluffing pleasure involved when one of these geriatric rust buckets finally crossed a 'professional' mechanic's threshold. In motoring's good old days, an owner would often have a rudimentary knowledge of what was ailing the crippled vehicle, and was able to cherry-pick from many of the necessary technical terms stashed away in fond memories of endless hours sitting at the roadside waiting for the AA to turn up to augment your motoring vocabulary. ('I'm sorry to say, sir, that we might be looking at a case of badly worn trunnions.')

Acknowledging that, for most of us, a 'trunnion' sounds like something a proctologist might investigate, Morris Minor owners will know better, although they'd also know that trunnion failure was preventable, by regularly squirting unguent into a small orifice.

Many period car bluffers would tell you that a trunnion is a spindle that sits in a sleeved metal casing called a stub axle, and is part of the front suspension, to which a front wheel is attached. It needs regular greasing to do its job, courtesy of a grease gun which squirts its lubricant through a suggestively named 'grease nipple'.*

Morris Minor owners who were too dim, forgetful or broke to get this done every 3,000 miles would eventually work out that the reason that their car's steering was stiff was because its lubricant-starved trunnions were seizing up. Eventually they'd weld themselves to their stub axle's innards and snap, and the afflicted Minor would pitch its blunt nose into the tarmac as wheel and stub axle detached themselves and ended up on the pavement.

* *See The Bluffer's Guide to Sex*

THE NEW ORDER

When today's cars go wrong, the faults are often more esoteric because a lot of the processes that make them work are nursemaided by computers. They oversee a car's vital signs like hospital monitors hooked up to an ailing patient. They decide how much fuel a car needs, how much air should be mixed with it and when all this should happen.

They live in dull-looking metal boxes called ECUs (engine control units) and have replaced antediluvian mechanical systems which couldn't finesse the combustion process required to meet anti-pollution laws. ECUs know how hot a car is and even how much oxygen its 'cat' – a device that concerns the exhaust system's anti-pollution equipment – has. It is also known as a catalytic converter, but not by people who talk frequently about cars, and therefore not by you.

On more expensive cars, there are computers that make decisions about how heavy the steering should be when it's going quickly, or whether the suspension should be jacked up or the car should hunker down on the road like a dog following a scent. They have firm ideas about what the brakes should be doing, if the headlamps should be on or not, and when and at what speed the wipers should be on.

Computers oversee a car's vital signs like hospital monitors hooked up to an ailing patient.

All these things are linked by great lengths of cabling, woven into looms hidden beneath carpets and flooring. These days not all of this is made of wire. Fibre-optic cabling is used and in some cases a single piece of this can send pulses and signals in two different directions at the same time.

So modern cars do a great deal of thinking. A lot of what they think is dull, but when they decide something's wrong the result is usually a bright, primary-coloured warning light flashing up on the dashboard.

The average car has a great many warning lights, and the average mechanic may not know what they all mean. Sometimes, especially if the car is German, it will shout at you as well, even when nothing is actually wrong.

Signs will flash up on the dashboard that say things like: ATTENTION! MY WINDSCREEN WASHER BOTTLE ISN'T EMPTY YET, BUT IT WILL BE SHORTLY, YOU IMBECILE. ATTEND TO THIS IMMEDIATELY BY TAKING THE CAR TO A MAIN DEALER AND PAYING A MINIMUM OF £1,500. NOW!

There might be a slight element of exaggeration here, but you get the picture. These messages are designed to either admonish you or to get you to spend vast amounts of money having your car serviced, and the onslaught of electronic admonitions is greater still if the car genuinely has something wrong with it.

Often these take the form of repeated 'bonging' noises and a selection of flashing warning lights, but bluffers should know the following when dealing with warning light anxiety when your car gets to the mechanic. If asked which warning light came on, there are usually three options: 'a green one', 'a yellow one' or 'a red one'. The colour of the one you saw last is really all you need to pass on.

A green light suggests that the car is telling you, 'I feel slightly off colour but it's not serious.' Yellow means, 'I am actually feeling really pretty dodgy and I think you should get me looked at.' Red is, 'For God's sake, help!'

Essentially, if you know how a traffic light works (and we sincerely hope you do), you'll find this perfectly comprehensible. The other warning light technique you can use is to point at whichever one has been flashing and say, 'That one.' Most mechanics understand this.

FEELING LIMP

One entirely modern piece of sick-car terminology, which you really need to know about, is 'limp mode'. This translates as 'it's still going, but not very well' and you can still hobble slowly to a garage.

So, should your car refuse to rise above 40mph, asking your mechanic whether it's gone into 'limp mode' is bound to make them look at you with new respect. The answer might be beyond the wit of man, as these days it's a process that often involves plugging the car into a computer, which will then ask a whole load of other computers what's gone wrong, and if they decide to be shirty and uncooperative or simply admit that they don't know, then the mechanic, for whom problem-solving is a forgotten art, will be stumped.

This is a case of 'computer says no', which is grimly amusing given that the equipment that has failed to solve the problem is known in the trade as a 'diagnostic tool', a term the frustrated car owner might feel could be applied to its human operator.

If your car has stopped, or is dragging itself along like a rheumatic spaniel, you really can't go wrong by asking the knob-twiddlers: 'Is it ECU-related?' Because it might very well be, or it may be related to the wiring that the ECU is connected to. So you will actually sound as if you know what you're talking about, and your repair bill might be smaller as a result.

RELAY RACE

Relay switches are another sure-fire winner in the non-specific fault department. They are little boxes containing mechanisms to switch things on and off, and they generally live in a larger box. Sometimes the bits that do the switching burn out, or stick, and quite often when a car gets old, the metal contacts between the relays and the rest of the vehicle get coated in filth or work loose, so the electricity that they're supposed to shift around decides it has better things to do than force its way across these dodgy contacts. Sometimes a repair is effected simply by waggling the relay around a bit.

SUSPICIOUS NOISES

There are, of course, some hardy perennial problems from which almost any car can suffer. The pistons that live inside most internal combustion engines have already been considered. These have two bearings: a smaller one called the 'little end' and one called a 'big end'.

If your engine runs out of oil and starts to make a horrible, rhythmic basso profundo death rattle, then its big ends have gone, thanks to its lubricant-free bearings having ground themselves to extinction. A higher-pitched clatter could be little ends, but equally it might be floppy tappets or depressed hydraulic lifters. What are these things? Don't worry. Knowing their names is enough.

BUYING AND SELLING

There were 34.7 million licensed vehicles in the UK at the beginning of 2018, and the majority of them had had more than one owner – or more than two owners, or maybe even more than three. That means there's an awful lot of people buying and selling cars, and if you're one of the former, it pays to know that a great many of the latter, especially the amateur ones, are really very bad at it. Their lingua franca is a sort of Esperanto of acronyms, clichés and duff pseudo-sales copywriting.

You can thank the Internet and sites like eBay for revealing some vehicle vendors at their most disingenuous, illiterate and insincere, because what they write isn't filtered by a copy checker, nor are they generally restricted on how much they can say. The result is often a sewage overflow pipe's worth of dodgy hyperbole.

The words 'nice', 'little' and 'runner', 'first to see will buy' or 'must be seen' should give you hives. Car dealers of all sizes and types often also come up with advertisements written with the speed and breathlessness of the 'terms and conditions' bit of a credit card's radio ad, often scrunching together vast tracts of information so that it makes no sense at all.

Then there are ads that try to bury bad news. One famously claimed that a car was 'immaculate' before mentioning, more or less in passing, that it had no back axle. Since the car was a Reliant Robin three-wheeler, losing an axle and both back wheels made it a one wheeler.

Sometimes you will need highly advanced interpretive skills to translate what the vendor really means. How about 'low mileage for year'? This sounds like a positive attribute, until you read that the car has actually got 115,000 miles on the clock, which is a lot, however you look at it.

'One-family-owned' sounds innocent enough, but it probably means that the car's interior has been trashed by recalcitrant children who've decorated it with projectile vomit caused by too many primary-coloured travel sweets.

And anything that mentions an owner's DIY styling modifications is bad, as a visually bastardised car is often an abused one. Speaking of which, beware anything where the vendor has proudly gone on about how fast it is. This could mean that it's been mercilessly thrashed every time its knuckle-dragging keeper has squeezed behind the wheel (cheap rally leatherette version with fake carbon rim, of course).

WHT DS THS MN?

Car sellers love acronyms. Look out particularly for ABS (anti-lock braking system, which stops the brakes locking); ESC (electronic stability control, designed to stop the car sliding about); EBD (electronic brake force distribution, an electrical thing designed to make the brakes work harmoniously, aiding the car's ability to slow down in a straight line); FSH (full service history). If you suspect that there are rather too many acronyms, it might be a good idea to adopt the policy known as DTIWAB. (Don't touch it with a bargepole.)

If you read the words 'no V5', then you should head sharply for the hills. The V5 is a car's ownership document, and the person selling it might not actually own it so, technically, you could be receiving stolen goods.

There's a shedload of other contractions and acronyms, but read enough car ads and they will start to make sense. It's a bit like learning a foreign language and suddenly cracking it. You'll see 'PAS' and just instinctively know that it's vehicle vendor shorthand for power-assisted steering.

Having got this far and identified a car whose owner can string a sentence together that clearly isn't a major work of fiction, you might decide to speak to them on the phone. Ideally the phone number you're calling should be a landline, but so many people use nothing but mobiles nowadays that this is a hard rule to keep.

There's no nice way of putting this, but when you hear the vendor for the first time, ask yourself if you're listening to a reasonable human being or a fool, liar or crook. Or all three. Bad vibes are nature's way of saying: 'Look at another car.'

And here's a tip from the respected motoring journalist Quentin Willson, who long ago suggested starting the conversation with the words, 'I'm phoning about the car.' If the seller asks, 'Which one?', that could well mean they're a work-from-home dealer but aren't advertising the fact.

Ask how long the vendor has had the car. If it's only a few weeks, ask yourself why, especially if they come out with something feeble like 'I just fancied a change.' No, they didn't. They either bought it to sell at a profit or they've discovered that the thing is a bag of nails and want to unload it.

THE ONCE-OVER

After navigating the choppy waters of telephonic sales twaddle, you will eventually discover a car that you actually want to see. When that happens, ask the seller to allow you to hear it started from cold. Vehicles that sound like a spanner in a food mixer when they're cranked up for the first time can often hide this when they're warm. If they're secret smokers – sometimes the sign of a worn engine – this nasty habit is most likely to be revealed at this point.

Arrive a little early. You might find the owner fiddling about with the car in a suspicious way. It also allows you the opportunity to look at the thing without the vendor breathing down your neck.

You don't need to know anything about cars to spot a bad one. If the paint is scratched and battered, the panels and bumpers out of alignment, the corners and extremities chafed, and the wheel rims kerbed, then it's been driven by someone who parks by ear. Are the tyres balder than Ben Kingsley? Are fluids and other engine unguents dripping underneath the car?

When the owner appears, have a look under the bonnet. You don't need to know what all the stuff does to see if it's covered in a thick layer of muck – a sign of neglect – or suspiciously gleaming, which indicates recent fettling. You should also be able to see if anything is leaking.

Arrive a little early. You might find the owner fiddling about with the car in a suspicious way.

When the car is cold, you can take off the radiator filler cap and see if there's water in there, and whether it's greenish blue – the sign of antifreeze. A lack of water or a sludgy mayonnaise-like deposit are both indicators of trouble (*see* page 65). At the top of the engine is an oil filler cap; take it off and have a look at its underside for more of that creamy sludge. If the thing is hard to remove then perhaps keeping the engine properly lubricated hasn't been a priority.

Next we come to the 'dipstick'. This is a thin, wobbly

metal wand with a handle at the top of it, which sits in a recess and measures how much oil an engine has. You can whip it out, clean the oil with an old tissue, stuff it back into its orifice, extract it again and, looking at the 'full' and 'empty' markers at the base, tell how much oil there is. If there isn't much, or it's filthy, black and grainy, it might be time to leave.

Moving on to the interior, if the car's owner has been prepared to drive about in a mobile dustbin, how have they treated the rest of the car? If the thing smells of old fags or cloying air freshener, these are not good signs, either.

TAKEN FOR A RIDE

You'll want to experience the car, which means going for a drive. If the seller won't let you drive, then there's no point carrying on. Assuming this is okay, and adequate insurance cover is in place, always invite the vendor to drive the car first. If they drive like a rock ape or white van man (much the same), make your excuses and leave.

When your turn comes, common sense will steer you through. If it has a manual gearbox, does the clutch start doing its stuff right at the bottom or top of its travel? That's a sign of wear. If, as you drive, the engine note speeds up before the car does, the clutch is slipping, which means it's on the way out.

Does the steering wheel judder when you brake? That's a sign of warped brake discs wobbling about. Are there any weird grinding noises when you slow down? That indicates that the brake pads that clamp themselves to the brake discs have worn down to their metal backplates and are grinding the discs to dust.

Do things like the horn, wipers, washers and other electrical gubbins actually work and, if they do, are the wipers making a noise like a cat scratching a blackboard? If so they're old and brittle, which is another sign of less-than-benign neglect.

Does the heater have a rotten-egg smell? This implies leaks in the system or a more serious mechanical problem known as a blown head gasket. When that happens the engine's water and oil are mixing and the result of that is either terminal or expensive to put right. The 'mayonnaise' sludge we mentioned that you might find on the dipstick and inside the oil filler cap also indicate this problem.

The rules of the game are simple. If the car looks abused and sounds tired, or if bits don't work and the seller starts coming up with guff like 'it was working earlier', don't buy it.

If, on the other hand, it drives properly, comes with a good service history, has all its legal paperwork, and the owner isn't a social inadequate and has a genuine reason to sell, then this could be the car for you.

TURN THE TABLES

Should you be the one doing the selling, then the answer is to avoid a lot of the negative stuff described above. But if your car looks like it's just come last in a banger race and sounds like a tramp having a coughing fit, then its appeal will be limited.

Cleaning cars is not one of the world's most edifying activities, but sprucing yours up a bit will help (don't overdo it, for the reason previously mentioned), as will having all the paperwork to hand and not trying to madly oversell.

You may well find yourself dealing with chancers, tyre kickers and people who try and beat you down on the price before they've clapped eyes on the car, or don't turn up at all. If they do turn up, make sure in advance that you've asked them to bring along proof that they're insured and have a driving licence. And whether you're buying or selling, not losing your rag, even in the face of ludicrous dishonesty, is always a good plan.

THE CAR SHOWROOM

Beware the car showroom. On the surface, all is calm. Plastic palm fronds sway lazily in front of the pedestal fans; complimentary stewed coffee gurgles by the artfully placed faux leather sofas; a plasma TV shows ad loops of impossibly beautiful people driving very ordinary cars; and your every move is being watched by a salesperson on CCTV.

When you amble innocently over to a shiny new model, linger a moment too long and he will silently move in with natural predatory cunning. Before you know it, he'll be at your shoulder, a cloying cloud of David Beckham Instinct eau de toilette enveloping you in a trance-inducing miasma as he whispers his seductive sales talk:

Salesperson I see that you're admiring the latest VeloCity Turbo SXX Cabriolet. It's unquestionably one of the best cars on the road today.

Prospective purchaser *Really? Why?*

Salesperson *(taking a deep breath)* Unlike any other car ever made, this latest VeloCity has direct injection technology, automatic double clutch transmission with paddle shift, low-rolling resistance tyres, sculpted turbo body kit with flared arches, 0-62 in 4.4 seconds with 465 nm of torque, giving a responsive and exhilarating drive, 11″ touchscreen media centre, velo-torque vectoring providing increased dynamic performance, interchangeable chassis control, power transmission by nine-speed manual gearbox or optional efficiency-enhanced Velociraptor Nippelkopplung gear change, and his-and-hers shaving mirrors.

All in all, this is guaranteed to ensure that you will instantly become more attractive to women/men, envied by every other road user, and more sexually potent than Errol Flynn in a 22-carat-gold E-Type. This baby's got more grunt under the bonnet than a Chinese pig farm.

Prospective purchaser Hmm. I see. Have you got one in metallic peach?

Salesperson Of course. Sir/Madam shows excellent taste, if I may be so bold. That'll be £99,995, not including tax. Please sign here.

But you haven't quite finished yet. You have still to broach the delicate subject of the 'trade-in', a euphemism for unloading the pile of junk you turned up to the showroom in. The salesperson won't want to take it (no one in their right mind would want to), but he's not going to let a sale slip through his carefully manicured fingers. At this point you should say the magic words: 'This needn't be a deal breaker, but it could be a deal maker.'

Salesmen love that sort of language. Expect to be offered at least £1,000 off the purchase price.

DRIVEN TO DESPAIR

There was a time when people who now claim to know about cars couldn't drive: a dim and distant prehistory when Jeremy Clarkson couldn't tell his clutch from his...(let's not go there).

After that came a period of knowing how to drive but not actually being allowed to and, before that finally happened, being officially taught how to drive.

For the purposes of this exercise, it will be assumed that you have no idea how to drive but would like to learn. Being able to drive is a fundamental prerequisite of the art of bluffing about cars, so let's start with the basics: the stuff that makes a car stop and go.

The average car has a steering wheel, which is self-explanatory, a gear-selection lever and, where it has a manual gearbox, three floor-mounted foot pedals which, from left to right, are the clutch, brake and accelerator pedal. (An automatic does away with the clutch, but that will be addressed shortly.)

Making the car stop and go needs a certain amount of coordination between these elements, and getting everything in sync requires practice. Initially, that practice will involve finding an empty car park or country lane, sweaty palms, a screaming engine and a bunny-hopping car. But after teeth have been clenched and gears graunched, these things generally mesh in some sort of harmony and the car will start to do what you tell it.

You'll have to learn how to use the other minor controls and the mirrors, so that other people know where you're going and you know where you've been.

At that point, you'll have to learn how to use the other minor controls and the mirrors, so that other people know where you're going and you know where you've been.

Assuming you're not at this stage yet, let's return to the clutch, which in a manual car is the medium connecting the engine to the gearbox, which in turn transmits its power to the wheels. If the clutch was like a switch – either on or off – every time this happened the process would lead to a lot of jerking and stuttering, which is why the clutch applies the engine's power progressively.

Starting from stationary with the engine off, having

checked the car is not in gear, you turn the key and start it, push the clutch to the floor and slot it into first gear, then gently start to bring the clutch up until you hear the engine change pitch because the clutch is 'biting' (not as painful as it sounds) and the engine is slowing.

At this point you want to give the accelerator a gentle squeeze with your right foot to make it 'rev' a bit higher again as you keep releasing the clutch so that the engine doesn't labour to a halt (known as 'stalling') instead of moving the car. You'll be holding the steering wheel with your right hand (possibly for dear life), so that when the car does start to move it won't roll into a ditch/hedge/solid object, while your left releases the handbrake – usually a lever between the seats – which will otherwise impede progress significantly.

Get that out of the way and your left hand can join the right, clamped to the steering wheel, as you stare gimlet-eyed at the road with Zen-like concentration, steer the car and prepare to change gear to go a bit faster.

This process is much as before, but involves taking your foot off the accelerator pedal first, excludes the handbrake and is faster, as you go 'up' the gearbox and the pace quickens. Going down it involves the same see-saw pedal movements as you shift into the lower gears.

Stopping means taking your right foot off the accelerator and planting it on the brake, but don't forget to disengage the clutch with your left foot or the engine will start fighting the brakes and keep trying to drive the car. A five-year course in physical coordination, under the personal supervision of an Olympic-standard gymnast, may not be enough to achieve all this with any guaranteed consistency but it should get you started down the right road.

TEACHING SOMEONE TO DRIVE

Free advice is worth all you pay for it, but if you're a parent or partner who's been asked by your loved one to teach them to drive, and relations are already a bit tense, don't. Get someone else to do it. Wars have been started over less angst and conflict than that involved in slipping into the passenger seat and uttering the words, 'Mirror, signal, manoeuvre' to your nearest and dearest.

Should you ever have conversations with the potential pupil that contain the words, 'You never listen to a damn thing I say!', consider how this will translate to being in a car with that person driving it in circumstances where one wrong move will result in death or serious injury (probably by mutual throttling rather than a collision).

Teaching someone to drive involves a combination of courage, recklessness, dishonesty, acting and extreme concentration. You will have to pretend that you're not desperate to wrench at the steering wheel, and that you're not about to have a screaming fit because for the fifth time you've asked the novice driver to look both ways before turning right at a junction yet they haven't, and it's a miracle that you haven't been flattened by a truck.

Not only do you have to assume an air of zen-like calm and not yank at the steering wheel, you also have to show the person you are teaching what they should do, while also having to anticipate what everybody else on the surrounding roads and pavements will do at the same time. If, on the other hand, you have the patience of a saint, and you're good at appearing relaxed when every sinew of your being is telling you to scream hysterically that you're all going to die, then go right ahead.

COMPUTER SAYS GO

Of course if people like Tesla boss Elon 'Mr Charm' Musk are right all this will soon be irrelevant because cars are going to drive themselves. Certainly a lot of industrial and personal capital invested by everyone from Ford to Google is going into making this happen thanks to a mix of video, radar, sonar, things that chuck out beams of light and massive computer power.

Driverless fans predict a traffic law abiding Nirvana of greater efficiency and reduced traffic jams thanks to autonomous cars bunching up like a line of dogs engaged in nose to tail social introductions. However, there have been self-driving prangs and fatalities, and one idiot Tesla driver was banned for moving into the car's passenger seat as he drove up the M1.

This technology is coming, but car bluffers might have cause to speculate that it will take longer to arrive than its cheerleaders predict, and when it does, if cars gain artificial intelligence and the ability to talk, will they be able to bore on to each other about the routes they took to reach some godforsaken out-of-town shopping centre car park?

There is a further observation which bluffers might think about lobbing into the driverless debate, namely, who is technically in control of a car with no human driver? Is it the owner, the registered keeper, a person using the car with the owner's permission, the manufacturer, or even the remote computer? Who or what is ultimately responsible for any driving mistake or transgression? Can the driverless car carry out an instruction to drive faster, or collect a passenger or passengers who have exceeded the drink-driving limit? These matters have yet to be addressed in road traffic law. Of course the bluffer is one step ahead as usual and need only remark airily that 'the jury's still out on that one'.

'I NEED ONE OF THOSE'

Car accessories have been around for very nearly as long as cars themselves, although the market for them has shrunk somewhat as cars are increasingly equipped with many so-called 'toys' as standard. But to hold your own in any conversation about the more risible examples, you need to have at the very least the following essential knowledge of the best and the worst of the extra bits of frippery that car owners over the years have convinced themselves are vital for proper motoring.

One of the odder early accessories was the 'Bosco Collapsible Driver', dating from around 1910 and marketed by one Lemuel Bosco of Akron, Ohio who, enraged after a $5 anti-theft device failed to prevent thieves making off with his car, came up with the idea of a fake inflatable driver to sit in it and frighten them away.

Bosco's blow-up motorist closely resembled Charlie Chaplin and came equipped with a hat and moustache. Despite claims that the mannequin was 'so lifelike and terrifying that nobody a foot away can tell it isn't a real, live man', the air went out of the inflatable driver business within a couple of years, and history sadly did not record whether anyone nicked one of Bosco's dummies as well as the car it was guarding.

When cars first got windscreens they came without wipers, so accessory makers were quick to fill the gap with clamped-on, hand-operated wiping devices that worked with levers or cranks. Some enterprising US accessory makers came up with automatic wipers that used a vacuum from the car's carburettor (the thing that mixed fuel and air before fuel injection). The only trouble was that the faster the car went, the less vacuum became available and the slower the wipers went.

During the 1980s, carmakers still sold cars without headrests. It was a case of 'pay more or risk a nasty case of whiplash'.

Carmakers generally used to be pretty mean about standard equipment and charged extra for items that today are thought of as essentials. Thus 1950s and 1960s buyers of small cars like the Austin A30 and Standard 8 would not get the luxury of a heater unless they paid extra, and when seat belts appeared many carmakers charged more for these as well.

Even in the 1980s the cheese-paring continued. If you bought a limited-edition Fiesta Flight in 1985 and wanted sun visors that swivelled to the side, this cost more than ones that didn't. And during that decade, carmakers still sold cars without headrests. It was a case of 'pay more or risk a nasty case of whiplash'.

At least by this stage most cars had heated rear windows, but since many 1960s and 1970s models did not, accessory makers enjoyed a roaring trade with stick-on demisters which, like many accessories, rarely worked properly.

There was a large market in extra gauges for things like Minis and Ford Anglias. These rarely worked either, but many drivers seemed to like having rows of them on the dashboard anyway.

And with many cars having headlamps with the illuminating power of ailing glow-worms, there was a roaring trade in 'auxiliary driving lights' which owners festooned across the fronts of their cars. Drivers imagined that these made their vehicles look like rally cars; in fact, they made them look like road cars with a lot of redundant, under-powered headlights tacked on to their bumpers.

Other reliable sellers included the clear plastic driver and front passenger window-mounted air deflectors, which had absolutely no discernible purpose.

External windscreen visors were another big hit in the 1950s and 1960s. These things both shielded the car's screen from reflections and ruined its aerodynamics. Weathershield would sell you a steel one that fitted a Ford Zodiac for £3 17s, while KL, a big maker of everything from aftermarket car heaters to seat covers, charged around double that for its visors, which had built-in car radio aerials that made little difference to radio reception.

In the era before airbags, there was a roaring trade in tiny 'sports' steering wheels, which the driver would grasp in a ramrod-straight posture with determinedly straight arms. These were almost as ridiculous as the 'square' Quartic steering wheels which came standard on a brand-new Austin Allegro. Oddly enough, Quartics didn't become highly coveted accessories.

Since few cars had headrests, you could buy 'clip-on' ones that fell off if you tried resting your head against them and offered no protection in a collision.

Front-seat passengers on more boy-racerish cars would often find themselves squashed into high-backed sports seats which looked a little like giant versions of modern child seats and were designed to strap their occupants in just as firmly and inelegantly.

The 1950s and 1960s were eras when cars suffered from chronic rust, and it was possible to rip rotting wings and bonnets from popular models and replace them with single fibreglass front ends, perhaps with flared wheel arches to cover the then popular 'Rostyle' sports wheels. In fact, plastic wheel-arch 'eyebrows' were sold by the shedload by accessory shops and are one of the few accessories that have stood the test of time.

Then there were the much-coveted alloy wheels. A bloke called Keith Ripp can be credited with helping to make these popular. The one-time sausage salesman from Enfield raced Minis, began flogging accessories for them and built a huge business called Ripspeed, selling bits that made all sorts of cars look lower and wider and sound louder. Ripp was also one of the first people to start selling the speakers and amplifiers that allow other motorists to enjoy a boy racer's taste in music before they hear his engine.

Even though he got out of the car accessory business some time ago, Ripp's name is still synonymous with the thud of bass speakers and gaudy accessories, as Halfords bought the brand name and began churning out a range of Ripspeed must-haves (which include in-car DVD players).

Bumper stickers displaying varying degrees of witlessness have been popular since the 1960s, from triangular 'flag'-shaped ones that let the world know that their owner has been to Devon or that they've 'seen the lions at Longleat' (but not, presumably, that they've had a baboon's bum on their windscreens, shortly before the loveable primate made off with the windscreen wipers).

There was a 1980s vogue for claiming that 'My other car's a Porsche', although strangely Porsche drivers didn't feel the need to invest in stickers claiming that 'My other car's a Lada'.

For a time, van drivers liked to entertain other road users with stickers that said, 'Don't laugh: Your daughter might be in here', which was never remotely funny.

This brings us to more recent offerings, including some rather clever ones favoured by older drivers in motorhomes, such as 'Adventure before dementia', or silver foxes in convertibles boldly proclaiming: 'To infirmity and beyond!'

Things that dangle and distract have a long tradition,

too. There are air fresheners, chains, phalluses and beads. Nodding dogs, a feature of rear parcel shelves for decades, continue to survive, although who invented them (and why) is not clear. Figurines that drop their trousers are a more recent innovation.

Waving hands with witticisms written on them are long gone, along with waving-hand Prince Charles and Lady Di cut-outs that car owners could stick to the insides of their windows. However, plastic eyelashes for headlamps and soft antlers for car roofs have filled the gap.

The idea of car radios can be traced back as far as 1904, but it wasn't until the 1920s that these became a practical reality. In fact, 1920 was the year Chevrolet offered an optional Westinghouse radio for $200. This was a valve-operated thing with its own suitcase-sized battery pack and an aerial wire that was so long that it had to be wound into the roof space.

Twelve years later and the technology had matured and shrunk, and American motorists had the choice of around ten car radios, at more competitive prices. In Europe, Philips in the Netherlands and Blaupunkt in Germany were selling radios for cars, as indeed was Austria's amusingly named Hornyphon which appeared in 1934, the same year the lowly Hillman Minx became one of the first British cars to be offered with a radio as an optional extra.

Car radios remained power-hungry and were quite bulky until the late 1950s, when transistors arrived. Soon the likes of Pye were offering transistorised push button car radios.

There was even a brief surge of interest in car record players that could play 45 rpm singles. 1960s customers for the Philips Mignon player included Paul McCartney, who had one fitted to his Aston Martin DB6; George Harrison did the same with his E-Type Jaguar and John Lennon is said to have used the one in his Rolls-Royce Phantom limo – the car with the psychedelic paintwork – to play Procol Harum's 'A Whiter Shade of Pale' repeatedly.

By the early 1970s, music-loving drivers were getting their acrylic flared trousers in a knot over the eight-track cartridge player. These things used bulky cassettes but had the potential to fill the spartan interiors of Austin Allegros and Morris Marinas with quadraphonic renditions of *Tubular Bells* and *The Dark Side of the Moon,* which would at least have the advantage of helping their occupants to momentarily forget what they were rattling around in. The cartridges' habit of jamming when the tape got old and grubby, and the arrival of the smaller cassette tape, consigned it to history.

By the 1980s, even the most meanly equipped cars had radios and as the decade progressed these generally sprouted their own cassette players. But there was a huge market in allegedly better players capable of letting the world know that your personal taste in in-car music inclined towards Duran Duran or Tight Fit.

By the new millennium, CD players with lurid, illuminated displays had succeeded cassette players, and a whole subculture, which became known as 'in-car entertainment' or ICE, was vigorously promoted by the likes of Keith Ripp.

Some car hi-fi obsessives buy kit purely to make a lot of noise, like American Troy Irving who, in 2003, equipped a Dodge Caravan people carrier with 72 amplifiers, 36 16-volt batteries and nine 15-inch speakers designed to blast out a single frequency from 130,000 watts of power. The idea was to create more wide-spectrum noise than a jumbo jet taking off. Apparently it succeeded, although worrying reports emerged that Troy's brain had turned to tofu in the process.

SPOT THE DRIVER

If you like people watching, then making a study of the sort of human characters behind the wheels of different cars will give you hours of innocent pleasure. Especially when you're going nowhere in a gridlock on the M25.

The types you will see are many and varied, but these are some that you will need to recognise:

THE LEARNER

Learners are easily spotted, not just by their L-plates (in which case they shouldn't be on a motorway) but by two other tell-tale signs: posture and expression.

Generally, learners sit bolt upright and stick close to their car's steering wheel so that their chests are often just centimetres away from it. This is usually uncomfortable, and forces them to adopt a stance like a praying mantis when clutching the wheel, which they will hold stiffly with both hands at the prescribed 'ten-to-two' position.

They will seem tense and distracted because they

are concentrating so intently on clutching the steering wheel that their hands never completely lose contact with it – another recommended 'technique' most of them will ditch for the remainder of their motoring careers.

The expression of extreme concentration will also be connected to a mantra-like reminder that they must theatrically peer into their rear-view mirror at regular intervals, work the car's controls, not drive into anything solid and answer questions about the Highway Code.

Often learner drivers will have their own little convoy of unhappy motorists, stuck behind them and becoming more and more demented at being forced to travel at 22mph.

Vehicle of choice Volkswagen Up! (very easy to park).

THE BOY RACER

There is an entire subspecies of new driver collectively categorised as the 'Boy Racer'. He will probably have passed his driving test at the third attempt, and is universally identified by a larger, louder and completely unnecessary exhaust designed to make his car's engine sound more powerful than it is.

The Boy Racer will usually be aged 18 to 20 but older, infantilised examples in their 30s can still be found. Oddly, not all of them will be single and their car of choice is – you've guessed it – a used Vauxhall Corsa hatchback in white, with three rather than five doors, as this betokens youthful, reckless abandon. A Fiat Punto or Ford Fiesta might also have the requisite 'meet-your-mates-for-a-race-at-the-B&Q-car-park' cool, but a Nissan Micra or Honda Jazz would not, as these cars are driven by your gran. The Boy Racer won't be seen dead in a car liked by anyone over 29.

His 'wheels' (as he will always describe his car) will have the smallest engine possible, because annual insurance cover will cost the equivalent of Haiti's national debt. There will be nothing on the car to indicate its engine size; but if there is, it is likely to be obscured by a lurid dayglo sticker shouting 'TURBO'.

The Boy Racer won't be seen dead in a car likely to be driven by anyone over 29.

The car will have lowered suspension. This is intended to improve the road-hugging qualities of a ten-year-old, 1,000cc hatchback, but will actually cause it to graunch its underside on speed humps and make it ride like a wheelbarrow. This will not deter its owner from fitting expensive alloy wheels and low-profile tyres, which will scrape against the car's wheel arches, thanks to the lowered suspension.

Standard lamp clusters will have been replaced by ones that light up like a high-security prison. Inside, an absurdly powerful hi-fi system will have been fitted, along with frying pan-sized speakers, inserted into crudely cut holes in the rear parcel shelf which will swiftly collapse under the relentless impact of decibels at a level beyond scientific measurement.

Vehicle of choice, but which he can't afford, Subaru Impreza WRX STI, with full body kit. You'll recognise it when you see it, and know to keep out of its way.

CAR CLUB COLIN

You can see them alone or in groups at car rallies, peering under MGs or pointing out to the owner of a Mark 2 Jaguar (who's just spent £25,000 restoring it) that the little rubber feet used to stop the bonnet battering the bodywork when it's shut actually date from 1968, and, since their car was made two years earlier, this is wrong. They are often called Colin. Not all of them mean to offend, although some do, and they are keen to impart this sort of detailed knowledge with people they expect to share their interest. They know exactly where a Ford Capri's bonnet stay grommets go, and you don't.

Vehicle of choice 1972 Rover 2000 TC Mark II, pristine in all respects.

MOTOR SPORT MALCOLM

There are also motor sports fetishists, who are closely related to Colins (*above*) in that they have mental filing cabinets overflowing with data about lap times, power outputs and who came 15th at last year's Le Mans. You will not be able to compete with any committed car enthusiast in terms of information retention and dissemination, so don't try, but if the really hardcore ones remind you, just a bit, of trainspotters, it's best to keep this to yourself, because the car-loving variety often has a pathological hatred of anything connected to public transport. Malcolm is of indeterminate age, but somewhere between 45 and 70, and prefers to be known as Malc.

Vehicle of choice 2012 Jaguar XFR.

COMPANY CAR GO-GETTERS (BOTH SEXES)

It's shiny, German and has a boot. It could be an Audi, BMW or Mercedes saloon, but whatever it is, there's something totemic about it for a certain kind of driver.

This is a male person aged between 25 and 45, an exfoliated, sports-loving, gym-going, team-playing, white-collar hunter-gatherer with an instinctive understanding of which executive 'saloons' are in, and which aren't – the sort of individual who gets a company car and is allowed, within limits, to choose what it is.

Rewind 30 years or so, and this person's dad would have driven a Vauxhall Cavalier or a Ford Cortina and been grateful if it had a set of rubber floor mats. Today, although Fords are often just as good as Audis and BMWs, and in some cases better, Company Car Man will desire something like an Audi A4, a BMW 3-Series or a Mercedes C-Class – because it's German and it sounds expensive.

If asked, they will also have total recall about which models are the fastest at getting to 62mph – a weird number, equivalent to 100kph.

The 0-62 thing is particularly important because ever

since male drivers were sperm, being first has mattered a lot to them, so arriving at 62mph 1.4 seconds ahead of your mate is life-affirming.

Female Company Car types can't escape identification; many will have formed close relationships with their male counterparts who can name every colour option on any German-made car. So if you see one in a metallic black Mini, don't expect her to let you out at a junction. **Vehicle of choice** BMW 3 Series 330e plug-in hybrid (male) Mini Cooper S Convertible (female).

SUV ON-ROADERS

Owners of large, luxury 'Chelsea tractor' 4x4s won't let you out, either – making it quite clear that whichever piece of road space you are occupying, they should be there instead. This is often particularly true of the outside lane of motorways.

Technically, such cars are known as SUVs, an acronym for sport utility vehicle, which is a curious description because although some of these enormous cars can be hugely fast, they are about as sporting as a steroid-drenched bodybuilder and as aggressive, image-wise. Their utility is often suspect, too. Although behemoth-like externally, some of them are surprisingly compact and bijou internally and trimmed with the sort of woods, cream leathers and pale fabrics that make their interiors as practical as mountaineering in stilettos, but no matter; such things are not what these cars are about. They are all about being noticed.

The sort of people who favour them range from self-made business types and well-heeled mothers, who need something the size of an industrial unit to take small children to private schools, to oddly coiffured Premier League footballers and drug dealers.

Owners of large, luxury 4x4s make it quite clear that whichever piece of road space you are occupying, they should be there instead.

Cars like the Toyota Land Cruiser operate in a slightly different world, occupied by people who need a hulking great workhorse to lug trailers filled with construction equipment or to lumber over fields to fix pylons or rescue sheep. However, the hugely profitable SUV off-roaders for the leisured classes are mostly coveted by those who paradoxically have no intention of ever going off-road with them.

For many big-SUV buyers, size definitely matters. And in Northern Europe – and especially the UK, where space is at a premium and there's less room for big cars – this isn't a deterrent.

Two models exemplify this perfectly. One is the BMW X6, a 4x4 that's about as big as a barn conversion in Surrey. It towers over most cars but has a sort of fastback 'coupé' body, the better to render it less practical and less spacious inside.

Then there's the Range Rover Sport. This is an exercise in aesthetic aggression, a car for people who spend more on designer underpants than most of us pay for our mortgages, a car that appeals to those who think a watch that doesn't resemble an airliner's compass is shameful.

Big-SUV drivers often seem to be unsmiling, bull-necked men of middle years who've made a lot of money in UPVC windows, or equally intimidating, strangely expressionless women with big hair and enough fake tan to coat a scally of WAGs.

Vehicle of choice Porsche Cayenne S 2.9-litre V6 twin turbo.

HARASSED PARENTS

These driver types may well be piloting a people carrier but can be found in almost any type of car with four or more seats.

If their offspring are very small then the vehicle will have a distinct aroma of childcare unguents, with perhaps a hint of disinfectant. If the children are older and have been joined by a dog, the car's interior will look distinctly furry and chewed.

There will be weary child seats, toys and weeks of domestic detritus: half-empty water and fizzy drinks bottles, crisp packets, bits of Lego for adults to kneel on when looking under a front seat for an inconsolable child's lost toy.

Peer into the inaccessible, dust- and fuzz-lined ravines between front seats and centre console and you will just be able to make out old, fluffy travel sweets glued to the carpet, from which a sugary syrup has leached and acted like a chrysalis around long-lost two-pence pieces.

Should one of these cars pass you *en famille* in daylight, look to see if the adult passengers are sitting in stony silence, or turning round to bellow at the warring/sulking/regurgitating children strapped into the seats behind.

At night, you will increasingly see flickering lights and images from small plasma screens stuck to the rear of the front-seat headrests, allowing the car's younger occupants to enjoy *Finding Nemo* for the 500th time.
Vehicle of choice Nissan Qashqai 1.5DCI N-connecta.

OLDER DRIVERS
Fast-forward 30 years, and many of those rear-seat occupants will have moved to the front of the car to make room for their own progeny, while their parents will have reached the sort of age where a car has ceased to be a statement and has become more a means of getting from A to B.

It isn't compulsory that this car should be a Honda Jazz, as there are plenty of other sensible cars that appeal to older drivers, made by the likes of Kia, Hyundai and Toyota. However, the Jazz ticks most of the boxes as the transport of choice for drivers of a certain age. Whatever you do, don't ignore this demographic reality. Pointing out that more than a third of British citizens are over 50, and that the car industry ignores them at its peril, shows that you have a keen grasp of which way the wind is blowing. We'll all get there soon enough.

A car for the older driver should have a high seating position, plenty of room to stretch creaking limbs, and big square doors for getting in and out. It will almost never break down, will be well screwed together, and will almost always have the option of an automatic transmission which gets rid of the drag of changing gear and stamping on a clutch pedal – and aggravating an arthritic hip.

Vehicle of choice Honda Jazz SE Navi.

WORD GAMES

One enduring problem faced by carmakers, once they've spent billions developing, testing and perfecting their products, is what to call them.

The trouble is that words that sound entirely innocent in one language have an unfortunate habit of coming unstuck in another, and there's no way to avoid the conclusion that it's the Japanese who've so far come up with some of the best of the worst ones.

Take 4x4 maker Isuzu. For years it used the Trooper name throughout its English language markets, but not in Japan itself where it was branded as the Isuzu Bighorn. There are many countries in the world where the proud claim, 'I've got a Bighorn' might well get you into trouble, but Japan clearly isn't one of them. Whether the Isuzu Light Dump, another of the company's products, is similarly safe from misinterpretation is unknown.

Then there's the Mitsubishi Shogun. A perfectly good name, with a strong hint of rugged Japanese warrior nobility, but for some reason the car was sold in many foreign markets as the Pajero (but fortunately not in Latin American ones, where *pajero* is slang for 'one who pleasures himself'.

There were also red faces at US car giant General Motors after it launched a car called the Buick LaCrosse in the French-speaking Canadian province of Quebec. There, *LaCrosse* has the same meaning as *pajero* in Latin America, but with the added twist that it applies to teenagers.

Somebody at Peugeot reckoned the world wanted a van called the 'Partner Tepee', without ever explaining why a tepee needs partnering.

Plunging deeper into the depths of unintended vulgarity, you should be aware that Honda calls its Jazz (itself a name with sexual connotations*) the Fit in some markets, but to start with made the unwise decision to also name it as Fitta in several Nordic countries, not realising that the word was slang for female genitals. Honda further compounded its mistake by marketing the car as 'small on the outside but large on the inside'.

Sometimes carmakers come up with names like Mondeo, which don't mean anything smutty because they don't mean anything at all. However, some nonwords have unintended comedy, and Mitsubishi is in the frame again, this time for Starion. The Starion was a beefy 1980s coupé and to this day its makers hotly deny that the name was an accidental result of Japanese tongues finding it hard to get round the word 'stallion'.

For its home market, Mitsubishi shed inhibition and offered a city car called the 'MUM 500 Shall We Join Us?' Nobody knows what this means, but Mitsubishi does not charge extra for the question mark, which really is part of its name.

Yamaha, makers of motorcycles and pianos, also knocks out a little minibus called the Yamaha Pantryboy Supreme, but then Suzuki makes the Van Van, and that's a motorcycle. Do not neglect Toyota's Deliboy and Toyopet, and Honda's Life Dunk deserves an honourable mention, too.

Somebody at Peugeot reckoned that the world wanted a van called the Partner Tepee, without ever explaining why a tepee needs partnering; while thousands of nervous French tradespeople drive Citroën Jumpy vans.

Go back a few years and one US carmaker offered the world the Dodge Dart Swinger – presumably with a matching fruit bowl for the keys. As for tempting fate, would you like to be the owner of an AMC Gremlin, a lumpy American hatchback. Ill luck with the Gremlin might well be the reason that the name AMC has long since vanished, and the same fate might be said to have afflicted German carmaker NSU, which disappeared in the late 1970s. 'NSU' is medical shorthand for non-specific urethritis, a rather private medical condition which can often be treated with antibiotics*. At various times it has also been possible to buy 'RSI'-badged versions of Fords and Volkswagens, ignoring the fact that these initials also stand for 'repetitive strain injury'. The Volkswagen Beetle had a military cousin, the KÜbelwagen, which became a familiar and unwelcome sight in much of Europe and North Africa during the 1940s, and 20 years later the model became a favourite means of transport among Californian hippies. Perhaps it's not surprising that its makers rebranded the civilian versions for certain markets, but you might have thought that they could have come up with a more inspiring name than the Volkswagen 'Thing'.

Gratifyingly, now that the Chinese are manufacturing motor cars, a whole new lexicon of accidental daftness awaits us.

(* See The Bluffer's Guide to Sex)

GOING TO THE RACES

Motor racing got under way almost as soon as cars started to work properly. If you don't have a fundamental grasp of the history of the sport, you won't even get off the starting grid, so this bit's important.

Despite its innate glamour and excitement (or maybe because of it), for much of the twentieth century motor racing was a shortcut to an early funeral and lots of people died taking it. Indeed, as early as 1901 the French government briefly and half-heartedly banned the sport.

ON THE GRID

James Gordon Bennett (who was a real person and not just an exclamation of disbelief) was the owner of the *New York Herald* and founder of the Gordon Bennett Cup, and also the undisputed progenitor of those who subsequently promoted the sport of motor racing.

In 1899 Bennett, who'd previously sponsored Stanley's expedition to find Dr Livingstone, offered a silver trophy to encourage carmakers to improve their boneshakers through competition. By 1902 the race he backed ran from Paris to Innsbruck, with cars like the French Panhard and German Mercedes – with huge engines and tiny brakes – thundering along public roads and frequently bringing their hapless drivers closer to their Maker rather sooner than they had expected.

ENDURANCE TRIALS

Many early car competitions were held over long distances to prove the newfangled automobile's durability. One was the Automobile Club's Thousand Miles Trial in 1900, involving a drive from London to Edinburgh and back. This was won by a raffish, handlebar moustache-twirling chap named Selwyn 'SF' Edge, driving a British-made eight-horsepower, four-cylinder Napier, averaging 12mph in England and 10mph in Scotland.

An Australian-born businessman, Edge was probably Britain's first celebrity racing driver. A clever self-publicist, he could be seen racing all over Europe and, memorably, in 1907 at the Brooklands motor racing circuit in Surrey, where he drove a 60-horsepower Napier for 24 hours averaging almost 66mph – which must have been exhausting, terrifying and boring all at the same time. The record stood for 17 years.

Brooklands was the world's first purpose-built motor circuit, with concrete banking 100 feet wide and nearly 30 feet high, over which cars would sometimes disappear with a scream of brakes (and driver). This was a marvellously entertaining spectacle which had the crowds clamouring for more.

AN UNUSUAL LADY DRIVER

One of Edge's protégées was Dorothy Levitt, one of the world's first women racing drivers, who was working as a secretary at the car manufacturer Napier and was by all accounts a bit of a cracker. With his moustache-twirling in full overdrive, SF taught her to drive and in 1903 she piloted his Gladiator car to a class win at the Southport Speed Trials, shocking society by becoming the UK's first female car race winner. Three years later she became 'the fastest girl on earth' at the Blackpool Speed Trials, reaching nearly 91mph in a Napier.

Levitt flew planes, raced powerboats and gave lectures to encourage women to take up driving, even though she wasn't legally allowed to vote. She was, it is safe to say, a hell of a gal – and should be a role model for bluffers, both male and female, everywhere.

GRAND PRIX GLAMOUR

The 1920s saw the arrival of events like France's Le Mans 24-hour race, which became and remains a huge party with an almost incidental car race in the middle of it. Despite Ettore Bugatti deriding Bentleys as 'the world's fastest lorries', the magisterial green cars dominated the event between 1924 and 1930, driven by a group of wealthy *Boy's Own* characters like diamond heir Woolf 'Babe' Barnato and Sir Henry 'Tim' Birkin, who were known as 'the Bentley Boys'.

By the 1930s the exotic caravan of Grand Prix racing was well established, and a lot of national pride was staked on how the cars fared. Many were lethally fast. The 1935 supercharged, 4.4-litre, 16-cylinder Auto Union Type B was capable of 171mph, but the car handled like an eel on a wet stone floor and offered little crash protection.

POST-WAR PETROL POWER

Almost immediately after the Second World War, the first semi-official British Grand Prix race took place on a bomb site in the London suburb of Cockfosters, and by 1950 a Formula 1 race with a drivers' championship involving petrol-powered gladiatorial combat between leading marques such as Ferrari, Alfa Romeo and Mercedes-Benz was up and running at Silverstone. The first title was won by one Giuseppe 'Nino' Farina.

Argentinean Juan Manuel Fangio was the man to beat in the 1950s. Driving for Alfa Romeo, Ferrari, Maserati and Mercedes, he was world champion five times (four in a row), never driving faster than he had to to win ('A crazy man finishes in the cemetery' was his motto). The dashing Fangio retired in 1958 and lived to be 84.

SAFETY ON THE TRACK

Other racers weren't so lucky. In 1958 the fatality tally was four, two the following year and another three in 1960. Drivers were being written off at a rate of one or two a year until the late 1970s, despite British driver Jackie Stewart, another serial racing world champion with three wins, campaigning for skilled medical cover, full-face crash helmets, seat belts, decent crash barriers and better circuit safety to protect drivers and spectators. Amazingly, he was criticised for taking the 'romance' out of motor racing.

In the 1980s and early 1990s some drivers continued to die, including the 32-year-old Canadian pin-up Gilles Villeneuve (described by teammate Jody Scheckter as 'the fastest driver in the history of motor racing') – but things still didn't change until Austria's Roland Ratzenberger and three-time world champion, Brazil's Ayrton Senna were killed within 24 hours of each other in San Marino in 1994. This led to a raft of not-before-time safety measures, and the average racing car is probably now safer than a parked Volvo with nobody in it.

Formula 1 still attracts vast crowds, vast sums of money, vast TV audiences and vast controversy.

A FATHER-AND-SON FIRST
You also need to have a passing acquaintance with British drivers Graham and Damon Hill, the only father-and-son pair both to have won the Formula 1 World Championship (in 1962, 1968 and 1996). But Hill senior can't claim the title of last moustache-wearing champion. That distinction goes to 1992 World Champion Nigel Mansell. There was a touch of Leslie

Phillips or Spitfire pilot about the raffish Hill, whereas Mansell, who hailed from the Midlands, often looked like a policeman – which wasn't all that surprising as his leisure pursuits included being a special constable on the Isle of Man.

MONEY-MAKING FORMULA

Formula 1 still attracts vast crowds, vast sums of money, vast TV audiences and vast controversy. Not every driver has everything from his underpants to his watch supplied by a sponsor, and not all of them trade in long-term partners for micro-skirted girl-band members and move from, say, Stevenage to a sun-drenched tax haven. But, of course, some of them do – and their fans would be disappointed if they didn't.

The bluffer's position should be that professional racing drivers demonstrate a unique mix of physical bravery, athleticism, coordination and single-minded determination which, in common with many other professional sportsmen and women, might make them wealthy but doesn't make them particularly interesting. Or likeable. Had their energies been channelled into, say, trainspotting, they might have been similarly dedicated, albeit somewhat poorer, but they might have had more rounded personalities.

They spend hours piloting cars that cost millions to develop and can hurl them from 0-100 and back again in about five seconds, but don't have to worry about their no-claims bonuses if they crash. At the Monza circuit in Italy the average speed is 245kph, but that's still 95kph short of the maximum speed drivers will achieve there. They will have their throttles mashed to the floor almost 70% of the time, and put their brakes on about six times per lap, but will change gear 46 times over the same period. They will be shaken, pushed and pulled about by the sort of G-forces fighter pilots experience, and some of them, despite being brilliantly skilled, will never actually win a Formula 1 race because the cars they drive are fractionally less competitive than the ones that win.

Perhaps racing drivers' existences, which seem to mix having very exciting lives with having no lives at all, mean that if they want to spend £2,000 on a pair of sunglasses that make them look like a twerp, nobody should begrudge them. But you can't help feeling that Nigel Mansell would have been much happier with a new truncheon.

NEW ENERGY

Racing cars are changing along with their road-going counterparts. An electric race-car series, Formula E, is claimed to have F1-style electric racers capable of 200mph that will reach 60mph in about three seconds. One car, the Lola-Drayson B12/69EV, has four electric motors that produce an eye-watering 850-horsepower. Critics wonder how long the cars will be able to keep going flat out – about 15 minutes in the case of the Lola-Drayson, which might reduce its chances of becoming a serious challenger at Le Mans.

Mind you, Le Mans itself has in recent years been dominated by diesel and diesel-hybrid powered racers and Formula E electric racing is growing fast. Who would have thought that 20 years ago? The bluffer's position should be that electricity will triumph in the long run, once they've worked out the technology.

US RACING

As ever, the Americans like to do things their way and so bluffers will need to be familiar with the names IndyCar and NASCAR (always in capitals) which are the biggest auto racing organisations across the pond. Between them, they sanction and oversee the majority of official car races in the USA. In world racing terms, they're a law unto themselves.

IndyCar

IndyCar involves racing in cars that look vaguely like proper racing cars, but which aren't nearly on a par with their over-engineered Formula 1 counterparts. Thus they aren't really taken seriously in global motor sports, whereas NASCAR can't really be ignored by anyone who professes to know anything about professional motor racing.

NASCAR

What you need to know about NASCAR is that it stands for National Association for Stock Car Auto Racing, and that it vies with F1 for the terrifying amount of testosterone it generates. In terms of television ratings in the USA, it pulls in more viewers than any other sporting event apart from the NFL (National Football League).

You'll also need to know that its heritage is soaked

to the very roots in bootleg booze. Indeed, illicit liquor trading is firmly behind the biggest motor racing organisation in the USA. To be fair, that's no longer the case (allegedly) but NASCAR is fiercely proud of its good ol' boy, redneck image. In the 1920s and 1930s Prohibition era, highly skilled drivers made a good living evading police while transporting bootleg whisky at high speed in modified 'stock' production cars across the Appalachian region of the USA. When the repeal of Prohibition in 1933 threatened to dry up their business, they began driving the still-illegal 'moonshine' – as dangerous as Irish 'potcheen' or the ethanol they used as fuel, and just as guaranteed to render drinkers (and drivers) blind drunk. By the mid-1930s it occurred to some of the better drivers that if they carved out a dirt track in a potato patch and started racing each other, people might actually turn up to watch.

NASCAR heritage is soaked to the very roots in bootleg booze, and it's fiercely proud of its good ol' boy, redneck image.

That's all you need to know about the background; these days NASCAR is very big business and while 'stock' cars might vaguely resemble standard production models, underneath the skin lurks a monster of a power unit operated by a beast of a driver, who is sometimes female, in full Kevlar armour.

You'll need to mention two races: Daytona 500 and Indianapolis 500, perhaps adding 'that's my idea of raw-seat-of-the-pants-racing-with-none-of-that-prissy-buck-passing-weasel-whining-I'm-only-earning-20-million-a-year attitude adopted by certain other professional racing drivers.'

One other thing you should know about NASCAR racing is that the cars only ever turn left, and so they are actually engineered with this in mind. And for extra bluffing points you might venture that they only race anti-clockwise because that's how horse races are run in the USA – apparently as an act of defiance against British colonialists who used to race clockwise.

NASCAR V FORMULA 1

This is always a spirited area of debate for bluffers, so try your luck by raising the following ten contentious points:

F1 is 'classy'; NASCAR 'trashy'.

F1 is boring; NASCAR is more interesting. Sometimes there are pile-ups of ten cars or more in the latter.

F1's worldwide TV audience is immeasurably bigger than NASCAR's.

In F1 the sprint to the first turn determines much of the race, outright overtaking is rare; in NASCAR the track is routinely three or four cars wide and overtaking is common.

Given a choice should one prefer to attend Daytona 500, or the Monaco Grand Prix?

In F1 it's all about who's got the fastest car; in NASCAR it's more about who's the better driver.

F1 is about finesse; NASCAR likes to get up close and physical.

F1 has got great looking racing cars; NASCAR cars look like something you really don't want to see in your rear-view mirror.

NASCAR drivers tend to be 'characters'; F1 drivers are automatons.

NASCAR drivers shout 'YEE HAH! F*** YEAH, BABY!'; F1 drivers address their racing teams in a dull monotone and talk about tyre pressures.

Take your pick.

Like people, tomorrow's cars will be battling with their weight and they'll come in all shapes and sizes.

BACK TO THE FUTURE

THE FIRST CONCEPT CARS

Cars of the future inevitably aren't. They're very much rooted in the eras when they were made, and while some were packed with clever ideas that subsequently became commonplace, other so-called concept cars are barking mad, or never worked properly because the technology and materials needed for them to become mainstream weren't around.

Take the Dymaxion of 1933. Created by the American architect, inventor and philosopher Richard 'Bucky' Buckminster Fuller, the man behind 'geodesic' structures, his car looked like an airship gondola, could seat 11 people, topped 128mph, was about twice as fuel-efficient as contemporary designs of the time, and was able to turn in its own length. 'It could dance very beautifully,' said Bucky.

It did this thanks to being steered by a single rear wheel (the two at the front were fixed) but this, coupled with a powerful Ford V8 engine, fairly limited aerodynamic knowledge, a body of light alloy and balsa wood, and a canvas roof, meant that when one crashed, a passenger was killed and the Dymaxion car project died with him.

If Buckminster Fuller's creation was the product of engineering purism, then the sinister-looking 1938 Phantom Corsair exists thanks to baked beans and a fertile imagination.

The brains behind it belonged to Rust Heinz, a member of the family that gave the world 57 varieties of tinned food. Despite not having any experience designing cars, he produced a prototype and persuaded an aunt to fund his huge, black, six-seater coupé whose styling mixed art deco with science fiction and looked like a cockroach. Capable of a then-impressive 115mph, the Phantom Corsair had front-drive, a 4.7-litre V8, push-button automatic doors, aircraft-like instruments and roof-mounted control switches. Advertised in *Esquire* magazine and promoted as 'the car of tomorrow', it appeared in a film called *The Young in Heart* as 'the Flying Wombat', alongside Douglas Fairbanks Junior. He – along with everyone else – resisted the temptation to buy one, and this extraordinary machine remained a one-off. Heinz was only 25 when he died in a car accident.

TUCKER'S TORPEDO

In 1946 automobile engineer Preston T Tucker of Ypsilanti, Michigan, came up with the Tucker Torpedo saloon. It had a 'flat six' engine in the back (a bit like a Porsche), developed from a motor designed to power Bell helicopters, a front-passenger crash compartment, a steering system designed to avoid impaling the driver, a padded dashboard, and three headlights with the one in the middle that swivelled with the front wheels – although wings that did the same and a central steering wheel were abandoned.

The 120mph cars really were ahead of their time but only around 50 were made. Tucker was accused of fraud and became embroiled in a lengthy court battle (which he won), blaming the big American carmakers for stitching him up. But by then the Torpedo had been sunk.

THE MOTORAMA

Tucker's hated rivals spent much of the 1950s coming up with outlandish 'future car' concepts of their own, many of which were inspired by jet-fighter aircraft and featured a panoply of fins and air ducts.

General Motors styling boss Harley Earl made up for frequent lapses of taste with a childlike sense of fun, creating cars that often looked as if they belonged in a science-fiction B movie. Many debuted at travelling shows called Motoramas, which ran from 1949 to 1961. The 1953 event at New York's Waldorf Astoria hotel attracted 300,000-plus visitors. Its star turn was a concept sports car with a fibreglass body called the Corvette, which GM would later build as a Chevrolet.

Earl's futuristic creations included the turbine-powered 1958 Firebird III, which looked like an aircraft fuselage shorn of its big wings but retaining several small ones guaranteed to cut pedestrians in half. Its two occupants had their own bubble canopies that could be raised using a 'sonic' key. A joystick controlled the car and, even more alarmingly, it could drive itself using radio signals from sensors buried in the tarmac of GM's test track. On a normal road it would presumably head for the nearest pylon.

Not to be outdone, Ford presented a scale model concept car called the Nucleon which, you've guessed it, would have been nuclear-powered. Fortunately, this car never got to the working prototype or crash-testing stage.

SCI-FI SUPERCARS

Generally, concept cars from the 1960s and 1970s looked a bit like mash-ups of spaceships and Ferraris. Italian vehicle design houses like Pininfarina and Bertone churned out very low, very wide and often entirely impractical supercars. Some of them looked fabulous but were wilfully impractical, such as the 1970 Ferrari 512 S Modulo which was so low to the ground that the only means of getting in and out was via an entire roof section that slid forward over the bonnet. It was described by its creator Paolo Martin as 'the craziest dream car in the world, the most unique, violent, inimitable and conceptually different.' He got that right. Meanwhile, Italian designer Giorgetto Giugiaro was about to unveil the Lotus Esprit 'dream car' at the 1972

Turin Motor Show, which actually made it on to the production line and later earned fame as the amphibian Bond car in the 1977 film *The Spy Who Loved Me*.

THE UTILITARIAN LOOK

The thinking behind some more recent concept cars is harder to fathom. Take the Rhombus, created by China's Changfeng College of Automotive Engineering. Its body appears to have been designed with a set square – all hard edges and straight lines. But even this can't distract from the fact that it has one wheel at the front, one at the back and two in the middle.

From the ridiculous to the sublime, some cars of the future do actually get built.

At least the Nissan Round Box had a wheel at each corner, but it also had a nose resembling an industrial vacuum cleaner and a tall, upright body apparently modelled on a Portaloo.

The Round Box is a vehicular oil painting compared to Honda's Fuya-Jo city car concept. Imagine an obese Dalek, shorn of its sink plungers but with sofa castors attached to each corner, and glazed with slit-like windows. Four occupants could squeeze in but almost had to stand up, but that's okay because the interior was set up like a mobile disco, right down to a steering wheel shaped like a DJ's turntable. Honda described its top-heavy creation, which appeared at motor shows for three years, as 'a party-on-wheels concept', one that presumably didn't include a built-in toilet for embarrassed guests to hide in.

ONE THAT WORKED

From the ridiculous to the sublime, some cars of the future do actually get built. Take the Citroën DS, which appeared way back in 1955 and had wind-cheating, tapering bodywork with a beaky front that either looked like a piece of mobile sculpture or General de Gaulle's nose. This other-worldly car appeared and caused a huge sensation in a grey, austere world that was still cleaning up after the war.

The car, which later gained swivelling headlamps, was so ahead of its time that it took Citroën 21 years to get round to replacing it.

PAST, PRESENT, FUTURE

This brings the bluffer to how real cars might really look in the future. Will they be little electric boxes, or emissions-free and hydrogen-powered? The short answer is that nobody really knows, so you can say pretty much whatever you want. Although electric cars can go further and faster than they used to, they still can't go as far as fossil-fuelled ones, which take minutes to refuel. Electric vehicles need hours to get fully charged and, if they do become popular, vast sums of money will be needed to rip up streets and put in the requisite cables and charging points.

And if they become commonplace, will men of a certain age stop talking about 0–62 times and mutter darkly about 'range anxiety', a term for how far an electric car's owner thinks it will get before coasting to a halt? This won't be very far if they dare to use juice-sapping luxuries like heaters, air-conditioning units and headlights.

Then there's the imponderable question of where all the electricity that will power these cars is going to come from. Will it just mean more gas and coal-fired power stations, or will electric cars have wind turbines on their roofs?

Some answers will need to be found very quickly, because every car manufacturer reckons that there will be a market for electric cars in the near future, particularly for city dwellers who might choose not to own them at all but instead hire them out from ranks as sort of pay-as-you-go cars like so-called 'Boris Bikes'.

ALTERNATIVE ENERGY

Bluffers are probably on safe ground by saying that it's only a matter of time before electric cars are the rule rather than the exception. Remember the early days of mobile phones, you will point out, when batteries were the size of houses and took 24 hours to charge, offering talk time of about two minutes? It didn't take too long to sort that out.

There are issues with true electric cars. Their batteries need precious metals that have to be mined, something that has an environmental impact, and the electricity they use has to be generated, some of it using coal and oil. Critics suggest this could shift pollution from exhaust pipes to power stations. Still, half the cars sold in Norway are electric, and in three months 142,445 electric cars, commercials and buses were sold in China. It's not easy to bluff convincingly about electric cars, however, because nobody really knows how important, or how successful they're likely to become. But with petrol and diesel engine bans planned (think 2040 in Britain), they just could be the future.

And what about hydrogen fuel-cell cars? The ones with electric motors whose batteries are charged by a sort of chemistry set involving hydrogen and oxygen going through a complex, entirely incomprehensible process (which only works under tremendous pressure) to produce electricity, and a lot of heat – partly explaining why the systems involved are so expensive. Making them safe and small enough to work in cars has proved difficult, but it's happening. Making a profit from them is proving tougher still, but you will knowledgeably point out that since the only emission that fuel-cell cars will produce is water vapour, it's understandable that so much energy is being put into refining the technology.

Meanwhile, carmakers are finding ways of refining petrol and diesel engines to eke out the fuel they use and reduce the muck they produce, so they're likely to be around for some time yet, perhaps in hybrid cars that also have batteries and electric motors to share or take over the workload. Some, called 'plug-in' hybrids, can be connected up to the National Grid and will act as electric cars until they're in need of a recharge, after which conventional engines will do the work.

Of course, batteries, motors and other electrical bits take up space and add weight, which is another head-scratcher for car designers. So, like people, tomorrow's cars will be battling with their weight and they'll come in all shapes and sizes. Whatever their automotive power, you can bet that, like people, there will also be a lot more of them.

ß

There's no point in pretending that you know everything about cars – nobody does – but if you've got this far and absorbed at least a modicum of the information and advice contained here, then you will almost certainly know more than 99% of humanity about how and when they came about, how they developed, where they are now, where they're going, and why so many people spend so much time going on…and on…and on…about them.

What you now do with this information is up to you, but here's a suggestion: be confident about your newfound knowledge, see how far it takes you, but above all have fun using it. You are now a bona fide expert in the art of bluffing about a subject of which the philosopher Marshall McLuhan once wrote: 'The car has become the carapace, the protective and aggressive shell, of urban and suburban man.' Sometimes it's useful to chuck comments like that into any conversation about cars just to see what happens.

GLOSSARY

Aquaplaning A nasty experience on wet roads where water builds up under tyres so that they lose contact with the tarmac and the car slides over it, exposing the shortcomings of ABS technology.

Badge engineering The term used for cars that are essentially the same as each other but have different marque and model names or have been slightly restyled. That's why Vauxhalls are the same as Opels.

Clinic This involves getting a still-secret new model and its rivals together and letting a representative sample of the public have a sneak preview to say what it thinks. The first Ford Fiesta nearly had round headlamps because a clinic's Italian housewives didn't like square ones.

Dampers The old-fashioned term for shock absorbers, used by vintage Bentley drivers and mechanics of a certain age.

Endfloat A nasty mechanical condition involving the bearings of an engine's crankshaft getting worn and allowing the crank to wobble backwards and forwards rather than just going round and round. The consequences are either expensive, terminal, or both.

Facelift Like the late Joan Rivers, cars are often given a stylistic nip and tuck as they age, in a bid to try keeping them looking young – and these are known to their practitioners as facelifts. As with the human variety, they can either be rejuvenating or unsettlingly weird.

Gudgeon pin Part of a car's engine that joins a piston to a connecting rod (if you've read the chapter on how cars work this will make perfect sense) and acts as a pivot. They're also the things the bells swing from in church towers. The name is said to date back to the fifteenth century, derived from the Middle English 'gojune', itself a corruption of the Anglo-Norman word 'goujon', which is also the word for a small strip of fish or chicken coated in breadcrumbs and deep fried. You need to know these things.

Horsepower Scottish engineer James Watt, the man credited with inventing the steam engine – although he actually made it work properly – coined the term 'horsepower' to describe the working capacity of steam engines in a world filled with working horses, and compare the relative power of both. Mine owners in particular wanted to know how many horses a steam engine could replace, so 'horsepower' was Watt's way of telling them. His own HP was about 1/20. On a good day.

Independent suspension If a car's wheels are connected to each other by an axle, when one wheel drops into a hole or rut the other jerks about in sympathy, impacting how the car drives. Independent suspension means that each wheel is sprung and attached to the car with a self-contained system. Generally it will ride more serenely and go round corners better, but it will be more expensive to make, which is why, even now, a lot of cars aren't fully independently sprung.

Jump-starting The process of starting a car with a dud battery by connecting said battery to another vehicle's healthy one with 'jump leads', then firing that car up and hoping that this won't blow up either or both vehicles' electrical systems.

Kinetic energy The energy of motion, which is of course central to what cars do and something boffins in white coats involved with vehicle crash testing understand. They know that when a car stops suddenly – say, by being driven into a concrete block at 30mph – anything inside it that's unsecured will keep going and, mathematically, the kinetic energy of those things will be proportional to the square of their speeds. Good luck trying to work that out.

Locknuts Car components vibrate, and many twist or move about, encouraging the nuts and bolts that hold them together to work loose. Locknuts generally have plastic or fibrous inserts that flex, allowing them to move fractionally without actually detaching themselves. Not exciting in the abstract but a big reason why most cars don't completely fall to pieces.

MacPherson strut Most cars have suspensions that mix metal coil springs and hydraulic shock absorbers. There isn't a lot of space for these things under a car's wheel arch, but in 1947 General Motors engineer Earl S MacPherson came up with the idea of combining the two in a single unit, creating a strut with the spring on the outside of the shock absorber, sitting in its own carrier and looking like a giant baby's rattle. No one has yet improved on it.

Neutral A position that the gear knob should be in when you start the car (unless it's an automatic, in which case it should be in 'P' for park). Also a useful position for the gear knob to be in when you've broken down and need to push the heap of junk, or have it towed.

Oversteer If you steer into a turn and it becomes a sharper turn than the one you intended, with the tail of the car sliding out wider than the front wheels so that you end up facing the opposite way to your chosen direction of travel, then it's safe to assume that you've just experienced oversteer.

Pimp my ride Slang for taking a tired old banger and tarting up or 'customising' it. Think lowered suspension, fat wheels, primary-coloured paint jobs and interiors kitted out like a Barbie Doll boudoir. It's not a good look for bluffers.

Q-car A term for cars that look ordinary on the outside but have been tweaked under the skin to make them more powerful that they seem. Comes from Second World War 'Q-ships' which were disguised to look like civilian craft but were in fact armed to the teeth. Also a description of any car caught up in the endless queues at the tollbooths on London's Dartford Crossing.

Recirculating balls A form of steering gear used in some cars. Also an accurate description of a car salesman's turgid patter.

Solenoid Lengthy loop of wire wrapped round a metallic core that creates a magnetic force when electricity is passed through it. Often used in things like starter motors, sometimes solenoid switches get stuck, but the average modern car's engine compartment is now so tightly packed that the old mechanic's standby of banging the solenoid with a hammer to free it up is rarely an option.

Tachometer The nerdy name for a rev counter. Not to be confused with 'tachograph', an instrument fitted to lorries and a useful way of recording the speed and distance travelled unlawfully by drivers with a fondness for amphetamine-fuelled marathon driving for a week or more non-stop.

Understeer Another handling characteristic that happens going round bends. This one takes place when the front wheels begin to slide rather than the rear ones. The upside is that at least you have a better view of where you're going and whatever it is you're likely to hit as a result.

VIN Stands for vehicle identification number, which is a car's unique signature and is usually inscribed on a little plate inside the engine bay. Usually impossible to find, even for thieves.

Woody Affectionate nickname for the Morris Minor Traveller, an estate car with wooden framing as part of its bodywork. Sadly, the wood had a tendency to rot very quickly, however much varnish or filler was used to stave off the inevitable. Dame Edna Everage, spotting one on a televised trip to Stratford-upon-Avon, memorably said: 'Even the cars here are half-timbered.'

Xenon Xenon headlamps are the high-intensity discharge projector beam arc lamps, particularly beloved of German carmakers, that give off a white light powerful enough to cause permanent blindness. Even when dipped.

Y-job Not an abbreviation for an indecent act that cannot be mentioned in a family publication, but one of the very first concept cars. This was a one-off 1938 Buick convertible with pop-up lights and an electric roof. It was and still is strangely beautiful.

Z-Cars Period British TV detective series that ran from the early 1960s to the late 1970s and featured a cast including famously shouty actor Brian Blessed and Colin Welland, who scripted *Chariots of Fire*. The programme was created by Troy Kennedy Martin, who also scripted *The Italian Job*, perhaps the most famous car film ever made.

A BIT MORE BLUFFING...

Available from all good bookshops

bluffers.com